THE VOICE OF T

Anne Netherwood

The Voice
of this Calling

AN EVANGELICAL ENCOUNTERS
THE *SPIRITUAL EXERCISES*
OF SAINT IGNATIUS

First published in Great Britain 1990
SPCK
Holy Trinity Church
Marylebone Road
London NW1 4DU

British Library Cataloguing in Publication Data

Netherwood, Anne *1943-*
   The voice of this calling.
   1. Christian life. Faith
   I. Title
   248.4

ISBN 0 281 04478 3

Printed in Great Britain by
WBC Print Ltd., Bridgend

With the drawing of this Love and the voice of this Calling

We shall not cease from exploration
And the end of all our exploring
Will be to arrive where we started
And know the place for the first time.

T. S. Eliot, 'Little Gidding'

Contents

Acknowledgements

Some of the material in this book has appeared in the publication of the Universities and Colleges Christian Fellowship of Evangelical Unions, *Christian Arena*, and of the Association of Christians in Planning and Architecture, *ACPA Newsletter*, and thanks are due to UCCF for permission to use this material. I am also grateful to Kathleen Innes who typed the manuscript.

Unless otherwise stated, biblical quotations are from the Revised Standard Version of the Bible, copyright 1946, 1952, ₁ 1957, 1971, 1973 by the Division of Christian Education of the National Council of the Churches of Christ in the USA, and are used by permission.

The extracts from 'Little Gidding' from *Collected Poems 1909-1962* by T. S. Eliot and 'High Windows' from *Collected Poems* by Philip Larkin are reproduced by permission of Faber and Faber Ltd and Harcourt Brace Jovanovich Inc., Orlando, Florida.

The extract from *The Story of Art* by E. H. Gombrich is reproduced by permission of Phaidon Press Ltd.

The quotations from the *Spiritual Exercises* are from the translation by Louis J. Puhl SJ (Loyola University Press, Chicago, 1950.)

Introduction

I stood in the car park and looked up at the building – four storeys of greyish stone built into the hillside which rose steeply behind. What on earth was I doing here? Too late for second thoughts now, I told myself firmly as the children clustered round to say goodbye and my husband Rob took my suitcase out of the car. There would be no phone calls, no postcards, no letters for the next ten days. I was about to begin an eight-day retreat, based on St Ignatius' *Spiritual Exercises*; and at that moment the two things I was most strongly aware of were firstly, being a dyed-in-the-wool Evangelical and secondly, having very cold feet.

The feeling of impending doom clung to me as we made our way round to the entrance. Fragments of schoolbook history floated across my mind: flitting black cloaks arriving by boat from France; Mary Queen of Scots and espionage; priest-holes and ancient bomb-scares in the House of Commons. The person who met us was wearing a blue pullover and grey slacks; not a black cloak in sight. He would be directing my retreat, he said. The children decided I would be all right and we said our farewells; the door shut behind them. This was it.

I had decided to come here because I knew I needed help. Rob and I had returned from working in Tanzania with the Church Missionary Society. We had thoroughly enjoyed our eight years there, but living in another country and sharing the life of a different culture had sharpened my own questions about the one faith which Christians from different backgrounds shared. I'd met long-serving missionaries who could remember the time when English Christians from two different English missionary societies working in Tanzania did not have anything to do with each other. It sounded like the Jews and Samaritans of New Testament times. But there was less excuse for us. Even at the time when the

1

missionary societies in the United Kingdom were beginning to pool resources and work more closely together, on the African continent we still seemed to be locked into historical conflicts which denied the gospel of reconciliation in Jesus. I wanted to get away and think about what had happened over those eight years, and find out more of what God might be saying to me through my own experience. There were still two separate Anglican theological colleges in Tanzania, one for Evangelicals and one for Anglo-Catholics. The Anglo-Catholics suspected the Evangelicals of being naive fundamentalists (and vulgar). The Evangelicals suspected the Anglo-Catholics of being crypto-Papists (and snobbish). I couldn't do anything about other people's prejudices, but I might be able to deal with some of my own. How better to get rid of the blinkers created by ancient party conflicts than by putting myself in the enemy's camp, and finding God from there? And if Anglo-Catholics were half-way to Rome, I'd go all the way to the Roman Catholics and see what happened.

I had toyed with the idea of coming to this retreat house run by Jesuits for nearly three years, but it had taken all that time to gather the courage to do it. I'd chosen this retreat house because the brochure said they welcomed people 'of all faiths or none', which I thought might be stretched to include Protestants. And from what I'd read about them and by them, I thought perhaps the Jesuits would know what they were doing. I'd met people before who offered others spiritual help, and some of them had seemed to me to be distinctly dubious. There are no Codes of Practice for spiritual directors; no Certificates of Professional Competence; no Registration Council to strike the unworthy from the list of those entitled to practise. But I thought the Jesuits had been around long enough to be tested by time. They have been accused of many faults by many people, but I'd never heard of anyone accusing them of incompetence.

The Ignatian tradition has been on the go for over four hundred years, and there are countless books about it and learned expositors of it. I knew next to nothing about St Ignatius, the founder of the Society of Jesus, and I knew even less about Ignatian spirituality. I had a vague idea that the Jesuits went in for an elaborate kind of prayer which only people capable of solving the Times crossword in ten minutes could hope to emulate. I had bought a copy of St Ignatius' *Spiritual Exercises*, but I'd got stuck after fifteen pages on the description of his method of 'Examination of Conscience' which ended with a table of letter Gs and little dots representing sins to be fought and conquered. Interpretation was obviously needed, if only to explain what the 'G' stood for.

I never did find out about the Gs. But I did discover that the Spiritual Exercises are a very carefully arranged series of scriptural meditations and what St Ignatius called 'Contemplations' of the Gospel. Over the centuries they have been used in the context of a long or short period spent in retreat to help people of all sorts to hear what God is saying to them now, through their past and present life as it is illuminated by the story of God's love for the whole world. Ignatius set out a way of helping people to open up their reason and their imagination to that love. Some teaching on prayer suggests that either or both should be suppressed when people pray. Ignatius believed that both were given by God and could be offered to him for his use, and that he could speak through them both, if people would only learn how to let him.

This book is not an amateur attempt to explain the *Spiritual Exercises*. It is a personal account of what an abridged version looked like to one Protestant who encountered it. I have used some of my own experience in order to illustrate what I believe to be true for other people as well as for myself. There is always the risk of being mistaken in doing this. I may have left out parts of the whole picture and thereby presented a distortion of the truth, or I may have wrongly identified some of my own experience as being of more general relevance than it in fact was. This is why I want to stress that the experience is only presented as an illustration of how God does speak in a retreat to a particular person with his or her own particular background history and character. An Ignatian retreat brings alive the common truths of Christian life which are accessible to all Christians through the normal channels of sermons, books, teachers of the faith, and personal experience, as well as through the study of the Bible. Anything I have written which seems out of line with that general truth ought to have brackets drawn round it and a large question mark written over it, and I hope that readers will do this for themselves.

Evangelicals have a bad habit of picking bits which appeal to them out of other people's traditions, like picking cherries out of a cake. The result is that none of the bits relate to each other. I have done this myself, and consequently had great difficulty in relating parts of my experience to each other. It is not possible to pick bits at random out of the retreat process; it has to be seen as a whole. I found that the whole tradition I encountered through that retreat set up deep resonances with the evangelical tradition in which I had been brought up. It also challenged many of my Protestant prejudices, as I became more aware of what God was calling me to be and do for him. The process seemed to be the same process of conversion with which, as an Evangelical, I was already familiar: allowing God's love to awaken my response and challenge me and call me on at an ever deeper level. I came away convinced that God is calling me and other Christians today to be willing to receive his gifts to us through each other's traditions, and that he can deal with all our prejudices if we will only give him access to them, and set us free to make available to others the gifts he has given us. I offer these reflections on my own experience in the hope that others like me may be encouraged to respond to the voice of this calling.

I should perhaps explain what may appear to be a sexist use of pronouns. In the interests of readability, 'he' is generally used as a common pronoun unless the context makes clear that it refers to a male person. 'I' is feminine and 'he' also refers to God. I hope this usage does not lead to any false conclusions.

1 · Retreat

'What are you doing here, Elijah?' (1 KINGS 19.9)

When St Ignatius wrote the 'Rules for Thinking with the Church' by which his *Spiritual Exercises* were to be interpreted, it was the Roman Catholic Church after the Reformation that he meant. My own earliest Christian influence was the Baptist chapel which I attended as a child and throughout all my formative years until I left home to study architecture when I was eighteen. The two traditions could hardly be further apart in their beginnings. Jesuits were responsible for reversing the tide of the Lutheran Reformation in southern Germany and throughout eastern Europe. The Baptists have their origin in a movement which even Luther thought had gone over the top; they are about as Protestant as it is possible to be. Their beliefs have not noticeably changed since their first ancestors met in the Middle Ages to study the Bible and pray in each other's houses. They are pious but deeply anti-clerical, convinced that all believers are priests before God; they deny that infant baptism can bring people to new birth in Christ; they sit light to the Church's calendar of festivals, and they dislike ornaments in church and vestments for the clergy on the grounds that the money could be better spent.

If Baptists were radical Protestants, Jesuits were radical Catholics, and the radical nature they both shared produced similar attitudes. Common to both movements was the conviction that Christian faith centred on a close personal relationship with Jesus, who was to be followed quite literally, whatever the consequences; their members were willing to die for their faith; and Jesuits and Baptists alike were fired with the missionary zeal which sprang from seeing their own lives in the light of the gospel. It was this gospel by which, they believed, all true Christian life must be regulated, and which will, if followed faithfully, unite believers through Jesus Christ with the triune God.

5

These convictions have persisted over the centuries. The choir at the church in which I grew up still sang 'Be thou faithful unto death, and I will give thee a crown of life' when I was baptized, just as the Baptists at the time of the Reformation had done, although I was not in the least likely to share their fate of being burned as a heretic. Retreats are still given based on the *Spiritual Exercises* as a way to help Christians enter more deeply into the mystery of Jesus living and dying for us. That is perhaps one reason why I found that there were real resonances between my own Christian past and the tradition which I encountered through the process of making a retreat. There was deep pain also, as I was faced with the real difficulties and differences which divide us. I believe that facing up to these is an integral part of living the gospel today. Like many Christians who long for unity, I have been tempted to reject my own Christian past because of the difficulty of reconciling it with the way God has led other Christians and the way he is leading me now. But rejecting my past denies his work in me from the beginning and the place he prepared for me in a particular family and within a particular tradition. My past history is the gift of God, however much it may have been spoiled by my own and other people's wrong choices, blindness and prejudice.

My family's piety was straightforward and down-to-earth. We all went to church twice on Sundays, and I went with my brother to Sunday School in the afternoon as well. I can't say I exactly *liked* Sundays: there was a rule that only 'Sunday Games' should be played in the short intervals between services and the meals which on Sundays were large and leisurely. What constituted a 'Sunday Game' was not entirely clear, so that there was some room for negotiation, but generally they were presumed to be quiet and were therefore, by definition, boring. I remember one particular rowdy afternoon when the adults descended on us to ban Cowboys and Indians. When the tumult continued my mother hauled us indoors to account for our disobedience. 'Of course we're not playing Cowboys and Indians,' I insisted indignantly. 'We're playing Old Testament Shepherds.'

I knew the stories of the Old Testament quite well, as our preachers scoured its more recondite passages for spiritual truth, which they delivered with impassioned oratorical hyperbole, and gestures to match, for forty minutes. We would discuss the sermon over lunch; I still associate the flavour of roast lamb with the question of whether the preacher was sound and his delivery effective. In the evening, the preachers appealed to us in even more impassioned style to accept salvation; we sometimes sang the last verse of 'Just as I am' two or three times if nobody responded by going to the front. My parents did not talk much about salvation, but they did encourage me to read the Bible in short portions each day, and I learned to ask questions about what it meant for me, and how to pray to God for understanding in the words of the Psalm: 'Open my eyes, O Lord, that I may behold wondrous things out of thy Law (Ps. 119.18). The Bible was God's law, containing everything anyone needed to know in order to be saved; and being saved was the most important event in human life. I would still agree about that, although I think I would now want to ask more questions about what being saved means and how it is recognized, and whether it is understood as an event or a process. In my childhood church there was no question about the content of 'salvation': you were either saved or you were not, and you knew when you had been.

My Sunday School teachers wanted me to be saved and I can't remember a time when I did not want to be saved myself. But somehow the whole question of personal faith became for me an elusive butterfly, gliding sideways out of my grasp just when I thought I had caught it. I was perhaps the kind of child who needs to learn by copying others and doing what she is told; I joined in activities and hymns and prayers quite happily when I could be the same as everyone else. My earliest memory of kindergarten Sunday School is a happy one, making models of Bible scenes in plasticine and sand, and singing an evocative verse at the end of the afternoon, which we called 'vespers'. Long afterwards I was still haunted by its twilight imagery, which always made me think of the small, high window in my grandmother's spare bedroom, through which I could see the evening star rising in the dusky blue sky. When we sang at harvest festival 'He paints the wayside flower, he lights the evening star' I knew exactly what it meant to know God as Creator, because I already had my own image of the evening star on which to hang my belief that it was God who lit it. But other aspects of faith were much more difficult to imagine, and ready-made images were a rarity in my church. However, I did believe in God the Creator, and I knew that he was found through a high window. Many years later I discovered Philip Larkin's poem which sets that same conviction against both religious tradition and alternative models of human happiness. When he was tempted to envy the new generation's sexual freedom, he wrote

> ... immediately
> Rather than words comes the thought of high windows:
> The sun-comprehending glass,
> And beyond it the deep blue air, that shows
> Nothing, and is nowhere, and is endless.
>   'High Windows', *Collected Poems* (Faber 1988)

Larkin's religious tradition of 'sweating in the dark/About hell and that' echoes the difficulties I had as a child with the problem of salvation. In kindergarten we were urged to give our hearts to Jesus. I dutifully said the prayer after the teacher, but I was never sure that Jesus had my heart. Why else did I have to keep giving it to him? In my family, it was polite to say thank-you and look pleased even if you didn't really like the present you had been given. But Jesus never said thank-you for my heart.

Later on salvation became even more complicated. There were no high windows in the hall where the Junior Sunday School met. It smelled of old gym shoes, and the superintendant had a red face and a bristly ginger moustache, and drilled our prayers like a parade sergeant. 'Every eye closed,' he would order, scanning our ranks to check that no eye was out of step. In Junior Sunday School we invited Jesus into our hearts. There was a Pre-Raphaelite painting associated with this exercise: Holman Hunt's *Light of the World*. It was one of the very few pictures to escape the ban on images in chapel tradition, and I was not at all sure that I agreed with what it implied. Jesus held such a very dim lantern in his hand, and the door he was knocking on was all overgrown with brambles, like the gardens of elderly ladies we knew who were too frail to tend them any more. If I'd been Jesus I'd have taken a chopper to the brambles before I did anything else, but he just stood there looking put out. The only other person I'd seen looking like that was my grandmother when she was being disapproving; it was a special look she kept for children who did not appreciate all the hard work their elders did for them. I loved Grandma very much and I loved going to tea at her house, when her big table with the lion's feet would be set with a lace tablecloth and eggshell thin china, and there would be two kinds of cake and egg sandwiches and perhaps shrimps and brown bread and butter. But sometimes instead of shrimps there would be home-made kipper paste, which took a great deal more trouble to prepare than peeling shrimps, because all the bones had to be taken out of the kippers before they were mashed. There were always little hairy bones left in, and I never wanted to eat any. Grandma's face when I told her was just the same as Jesus's face in the picture.

How do you let Jesus into your heart? The door in the picture had no knob on the outside, we were told, because it has to be opened from within. But was opening it merely a question of turning a knob on the door? Years later, I went on holiday with some friends to Turkey and visited the great Saracen castle outside Istanbul, with its massive fortifications in row upon row of concentric rings. In my experience, letting God into my life is much more like siege warfare than Holman Hunt's picture would suggest. Other people have found this, including ᴧe poet John Donne, who took his imagery from contemporary scenes of a besieged town:

> Batter my heart, three-personed God, for you
> As yet but knock, breathe, shine, and seek to mend;
> That I may rise and stand, o'erthrow me and bend
> Your face to break, blow, burn and make me new.
> I, like a usurped town to another due,
> Labour to admit you, but O, to no end...
> 'Holy Sonnets', XIV

That is an image of my defensive resistance to God's entry into my deepest life. But my childhood images of warfare were, apart from the odd skirmish between different parties of Old Testament shepherds, the Soldiers of Christ who fought on God's side. I loved stories of King Arthur's knights and their long quests and adventures, and I loved my children's hymnbook with its pictures of angels with golden wings and knights in armour who fought under a great white banner emblazoned with a red cross. Grandpa, who played the organ in church, would pull out the trumpet stop, and I would sing with the rest of the congregation at the top of my voice:

> March we forth in the strength of God
> With the banner of Christ unfurled,
> That the light of the glorious Gospel of truth
> May shine throughout the world...

To my great delight, Grandma had the banner of Christ in her garage, which she let me play with when we visited her. I would hold it high and charge off to find the Holy Grail, followed by my small brother whom I rescued from innumerable dragons until he grew too old to agree any more to be the fair maiden. Sometimes I fought under the banner of Christ, and sometimes it was the Union Jack which was rolled up with it in the garage. Perhaps neither Grandma nor I distinguished any too sharply between them.

I have described these images of early childhood at some length because I have found that they represent ways of understanding my life with God. A formal retreat begins with the invitation to go back to the past, distorted and blurred as it is in memory, and find in it significant points which were good and true. These can function as fixed sights from which to take bearings as I search for the true springs of faith in order to draw on them as a permanent source of strength in my present life. This is what God's people have always had to do. The Israelites recited the fixed points of their early journey with God every time they came to present the firstfruits of their harvest:

> A wandering Aramaean was my father;
> and he went down to Egypt and sojourned there, few in number;
> and there he became a nation, great, mighty, and populous,
> and the Egyptians treated us harshly, and afflicted us,
> and laid upon us hard bondage.
> Then we cried to the Lord, the God of our fathers,

and the Lord heard our voice, and saw our affliction,
our toil and our oppression;
and the Lord brought us out of Egypt with a mighty hand
and an outstretched arm,
with great terror, with signs and wonders;
and he brought us into this place...
   (Deut. 26. 5-9)

The story begins with a journey into the unknown, a time of prosperity in exile from the land of promise, and a time of growing affliction, before ever God's people begin to cry to him in earnest. The prophets constantly reminded the people of Israel of the patterns of God's meeting with them in the past, in their own history, so that they would be able to recognize the true significance of what was happening in the present and take the right direction in the future. The people's resistance to the prophets' message sprang from the same prejudices which close my mind to what God is saying to me. They were condemned for their unbelief, their false gods, and their vain efforts to create their own system of security apart from God by entering into political alliances with the great powers of their time. And like them I can think I am fighting the Lord's battles, when all the time I am fighting against him as he comes to meet me. Like Israel who failed to respond to God in her national life, so I fail to respond to him in my personal life. My faith is often a very thin layer on the surface of a vast sea of unbelief, like ice which may look solid but will not bear my weight when I step out on it. I have false gods and false images of the one true God just as Israel did, even if mine are not sculpted in gold as theirs were. And I constantly draw back from the challenges of living in faith, and try to rely on alternative models of security which I can share with people in the society around me without embarrassing them by mentioning God.

Because there are real correspondences between my own life and the life of God's people in the past, I can learn from the whole Bible even if I read it simply as the story of God's encounter with people whom he loved and called into a relationship with himself. But when I begin to recognize the patterns of response in faith and unbelief which are repeated throughout the history of Israel and of

11

the Church, and see them as patterns which repeat also in my life, then I can enter into the story at a deeper level and let it wake echoes in my own experience. Praying with the Bible is a way of listening to these echoes and allowing them to speak to me in a voice which I can recognize as God's. That is the reason for going away on retreat. Like Elijah I can make a journey to a place where God has spoken before to his people in the hope that he will speak to me and that I may there be able to recognize his voice clearly. He may speak to me as he spoke to Elijah: not in torrents of fire and thunder and whirlwind but in a small, insignificant murmur which I might easily miss if I were not listening closely. And what he says may be extremely revolutionary - to me as it was to Elijah.

High windows and stars to guide and angels and knights who fought under Christ's banner were the fixed points of my childhood faith, and they were all images: true images, but images none the less. The journey from image to reality is a journey like the journeys in the Bible, where there are real messengers of God who may or may not be recognized, guiding lights, fleeting glimpses of the journey's goal, and battles with enemies. Images can lead to dead ends, like fantasy games where a wrong turning can lead to annihilation with the message 'your adventure ends here'. But the real Christian journey is made in the middle of ordinary daily life, in the faith of the resurrection of Jesus Christ which assures me that my adventure will only end in the life which has no end where, as St Augustine said:

> Then shall we know this thing perfectly, and we shall
> perfectly rest and shall perfectly see that He is God...
> There we shall rest and see, we shall see and love, we
> shall love and we shall praise. Behold what shall be in the
> end without end! For what other thing is our end,
> but to come to that kingdom of which there is no end?
> *City of God* 22:30

Until then the way is not always at all clear. A retreat is an opportunity to take time away from external distractions in order to hear God again; an Ignatian retreat links the process explicitly with the story of all God's people, through the Bible. An individually - given retreat is an opportunity to share one's own present journey with someone else who is also listening to what God is saying through it and who can suggest appropriate parts of Scripture to reinforce God's particular word for this time and place. But that is a subject in itself, which the next chapter will explore.

2 · Spiritual Direction

Your ears shall hear a word behind you, saying, 'This is the way, walk in it' (ISAIAH 30.21)

Spiritual direction in the context of a retreat is a particular form of spiritual direction in general. It is limited by the fact that the retreat-giver and the retreatant do not usually know each other, and also by the limited time they spend together: usually about half an hour each day. I shall give some examples of the wider, general sense of spiritual direction in this chapter, and link my own experience of this kind of help with the much more specific help given in a guided retreat. In its widest meaning, spiritual direction is the help, advice and encouragement which people give to each other in their daily experience of living in faith. This is, of course, a normal part of all Christian life and not at all a specialist preserve.

Many people *have* understood spiritual direction as rather a specialist preserve, however, partly because the assumptions we make about how God guides us affect our ideas about how other people can help us to him – and perhaps about which people can help us. God's guidance is a tricky subject and people have come to grief before now when dealing with it. One of these was Caravaggio, a painter in Italy who worked around 1600 and whose story is told by E. H. Gombrich:

> He was given the task of painting a picture of St Matthew for the altar of a church in Rome. The Saint was to be represented writing the gospel, and, to show that the gospels were the word of God, an angel was to be represented inspiring his writings. Caravaggio, who was a very earnest and uncompromising young artist, thought hard about what it must have been like when an elderly, poor, working man, a simple publican, suddenly had to sit down to write a book. And so he painted a picture of St Matthew with a bald head and bare, dusty feet, awkwardly

14

gripping the huge volume, anxiously wrinkling his brow under the unaccustomed strain of writing. By his side he painted a youthful angel, who seems just to have arrived from on high, and who gently guides the labourer's hand as a teacher may do to a child. When Caravaggio delivered this picture to the church where it was to be placed on the altar, people were scandalized at what they took to be lack of respect for the Saint. The painting was not accepted, and Caravaggio had to try again. This time he took no chances. He kept strictly to the conventional ideas of what an angel or Saint should look like.

The Story of Art, Phaidon 1950 (fifteenth edn 1989), p. 12f

Caravaggio's second attempt shows a silvery-haired, aristocratic-looking gentleman sitting with quill poised and eyes piously raised to the top right-hand corner of the room where the angel hovers just below the ceiling to dictate.

That story delighted my father, who first read it to me when I was having my own problems with the religious conventions in which I had been brought up. Rather than the committee who had made him conform, I wanted Caravaggio to be right; but was he? Leaving aside questions of artistic composition as well as those of New Testament scholarship, Caravaggio's two paintings express two different ways of understanding how God guides people. The conventional view is that God reserves his inspiration for special occasions, like writing Scripture, and for specially chosen people, like the twelve apostles. The revolutionary view is that ordinary, working people can expect God to reveal his truth to them whenever they set out to obey him by undertaking a particular task which only they can do.

I think the revolutionary view is the true one. Renewal movements seem to begin in very similar ways, when people are drawn to read the Scriptures with their eyes open and find that the text comes alive and speaks the word of God to them for their own time and place. Nobody can make this happen or control the results. I know a respectable Old Testament lecturer who was thrown out of the country where he was working when his students began to read the book of Exodus and found that it resonated with their own experience of living under a repressive political regime. Pressure to conform is not usually as obvious as that, but Christian convention may stifle renewal perhaps even more effectively than outright opposition by a hostile government.

Convention usually speaks with the voice of common sense and reason, and it is perfectly true that renewal is a dangerous business. Reformers may be rejected by their own organization or even by the Church as a whole, and when this happens they may find themselves heading a schism. Renewal movements may mistake siren voices for the prompting of the Holy Spirit and end in heresy of one sort or another. Individuals may come to believe themselves to be beyond correction or need of advice, and Christian history is littered with the sad remains of such folk. Renewal implies growth and movement, and people who are growing are vulnerable: growth can be stunted or warped. People on the move can take a wrong turning. It is only armchair travellers who never hold the map upside-down. Spiritual direction is needed whenever people are growing or on the move. I need a human angel with both feet firmly on the floor to check that my growth is balanced, and to encourage me to follow God's leading outside the limits of my conventional Christian response. Often the angel is quite close at hand and I do not even realize that I have received 'spiritual direction' until some while later.

My mother and father were my first spiritual guides. Like most conscientious parents they tried to guide their children in the right way, but they may not have realized what for me was the most significant and lasting formation which they gave. Between them they corrected the bias in our particular tradition which could give the unwary the impression that faith was divorced from ordinary life and opposed to the normal processes of human activity and thought. Mother would pack up a picnic and take us on a bus to the woods where we would look for different kinds of flowers and birds. She knew the names of most of them, as well as the trees which she showed us how to recognize in summer or winter. She passed on to us her own enthusiasm for nature. I still watch for the sticky buds to break into green on the horse chestnut trees, and I still notice the colour of shadows. Mother captured that distinctive

16

quality of light in her water-colour painting; it was one way of celebrating her enjoyment of God's creation. I never doubted that it was God who was to be thanked for the smell of the seaweed and the taste of salt rain on my face as I walked along the beach in January, listening to the high, wild cry of seagulls sliding down the wind.

Mother never spoke much about her own experience of God, but I knew without her telling me that spiritual life came from the same God who created the world that I could see and enjoy. I had a firm, if unarticulated, conviction that there could be no false separation of religious life from the rest of my life, and no 'spiritual life' that had nothing to do with physical life in the world. When I was at secondary school we sang a hymn in the school hymn-book which expressed that conviction perfectly:

> Set in my heart thy love I find;
> My wandering mind
> To Thee thou leadest:
> My trembling hope, my strong desire
> With heavenly fire
> Thou kindly feedest.
> Lo, all things fair
> Thy path prepare,
> Thy beauty to my spirit calleth…
>   Robert Bridges, 'Thee Will I Love'

That hymn was also in the hymn-book we used at chapel, I discovered, but we never sang it, and it was not the way that chapel convention preferred to think of as the way to God. But it was a way that I could recognize myself. I knew what that verse meant as I never did know the meaning of some of the hymns we sang in church, expressing emotions that have no echo in my own experience. But those other hymns did serve to remind me that my own experience is not the only experience there is. The truth I knew then, that creation can lead me to God, may itself become convention.

It is possible to insist on the beauty of God to such an extent that human ugliness is set in opposition to the glories of wild nature.

17

This may lead to a form of religious romanticism which finds God on mountain tops but never in cities. It may even ignore the whole truth of the gospel, that the Word was made flesh and lived among us, and men saw the glory of God not in sunsets but in the person of a village carpenter. Because I do find God in the beauties of nature I am particularly prone to that romantic error, which will raise its head again later. But that verse of the hymn I sang at school is saved from mere romanticism by the last lines:

> Thine to remain
> In joy or pain,
> And count it gain
> Whate'er befalleth.

I have had to learn, stumbling and fainthearted, the truth that if I dare to trust myself to God he will provide the correction I need, in whatever form is best for me. That may sound fatalistic. I think it is not, because of the struggles I have had, and still have, to accept it. But the first presentation of faith I met at chapel did seem fatalistic, and that fatalism was blown apart by my father's cheerful scepticism.

Father took me sailing. He taught me the rules of safety at sea; he made me wear a life-jacket, and he showed me how to head the dinghy into the wind and trim the sails and use my own weight to balance the boat so that it did not capsize, as well as how to right it if it did. He showed me how to reduce sail area in a strong wind, and taught me how to tell when the wind was too high for our little boat to be safely sailed at all. For every hour we spent sailing down the estuary in summer, we seemed to put in at least ten in maintenance: scraping, painting, varnishing, and renewing tackle. I would sit in church and listen to the Sunday sermon, my hands still red from Saturday's sandpaper, and wonder greatly about the conventional and often repeated illustration of faith. Faith, it was suggested, was like stepping into a boat and trusting it would carry you across the river. But we never simply stepped into our boat. Everything that could be checked was checked and re-checked before we set sail, and whatever we couldn't see then we examined exhaustively when we laid the boat up on the landing stage for the winter. My father would laugh and say that whoever thought of that illustration didn't know much about boats. It occurred to me that perhaps he didn't know everything there was to know about faith either.

People who had been brought up as Anglicans sometimes joined our church. They often said that they found freedom and true faith there. My journey led me in the opposite direction. I needed to base my faith on something other than my own religious emotion. For me emotion comes at the end of the process of learning about God, not at the beginning. Chapel convention scoffed at a religion based on mere creeds: it sang hymns about the religion of the heart. I needed creeds as a starting point in order to come to a true response with my heart. But all that lay in the future. My father helped me through my first struggles with chapel convention by insisting that reason and faith were not mutually exclusive, and that science could be studied without jeopardizing Christian belief. 'All truth is God's,' he would repeat. 'Nobody need be afraid of awkward facts. Just check that they are indeed facts, though, as far as you can.' It was good advice at a time when I was enjoying school life and learning, and wondering how it all fitted in with a convention which stressed the dangers of thinking as an obstacle to true faith in God.

Later on I discovered that there were limits to reason. Trusting in my own thought processes was far too like trusting in myself to be altogether healthy. I still do believe that God made our brains, and he made them for us to use, not for us to pickle in formalin and rely solely on our feelings or our imaginations. That belief has helped me withstand the beguiling invitations both of enthusiastic charismatics who have promised direct guidance from God for every detail of life down to choosing a new pair of shoes, and of starry-eyed mystics who undertook to expound the spiritual significance of every last flicker of dream and fantasy. But rationalism can be just as much a one-sided convention as those more obvious dangers of equating what is spiritual with what is irrational. I have had to reflect rationally on irrational experiences which might or might not come from God. I have also needed the warning a wise person gave me, not to over-repress any emphasis

19

on experience and awareness of God. Experience of God is not dangerous, he wrote; prudence can be overdone. Western Christians can be far too inhibited: 'The Eastern tradition roots all theology itself in the direct experience of God, and is far more open to the possibility of our being possessed by the Holy Spirit. Indeed, such a possession becomes the true object and theme of prayer, the fulfilment of our penitent surrender to God... Beware of too much restraint!' That advice echoed another verse of that hymn I had sung at school:

> Since but in thee
> I can go free
> From earthly care and vain oppression,
> This prayer I make
> For Jesus' sake
> That thou me take
> In thy possession.

The whole aim of spiritual direction of whatever sort is to help a person transfer the ownership and control of his deepest centre into God's hands. Restraint and reason may be one more circle of defence against God which I use to keep in control of my own life. This is why renewal movements are sometimes accompanied by people losing control of themselves: sobbing, or fainting, or otherwise being carried away. The dangers of excess and attention-seeking are obvious, but it may well be that God can overcome the deeper defences in some people only by some such drastic means. Spiritual guidance is even more necessary when this happens. Just as major surgical operations require the skill of an experienced consultant, so deep spiritual change needs to be guided by someone who is not only prayerful but also competent. If such a person is not available it may be wiser to wait.

I am rather wary of prayer groups which encourage their members to open up their deepest secrets to relative strangers. Love of God is, like a lily bulb, planted deep. It needs to be left to root undisturbed. The image of a castle is a good image of protective enclosure as well as of the wrong sort of defence. I may use my natural defences mistakenly against God's own entry into my life.

But that is no good reason for removing them altogether. One of the most frequent images of growth in the Bible is the image of a vineyard; and vineyards had walls as well as support for the vines.

Images of growth in the Gospels illustrate the further truth that spiritual growth, like natural growth, cannot be forced without weakening the plant. A spiritual director is quite unable to *make* people grow in faith and love, however much he might see the need for them to do so. He can only do what a good gardener does: notice the signs of soil deficiency, weeds or pests and suggest corrective measures; notice the natural habits of plants and suggest the conditions in which they will grow best.

Some parables in the Gospels compare God to a gardener, but others suggest that spiritual guides are like tenant farmers. The parable of the wicked tenants may have been told to remind the leaders of the first-century Jews that God's people belong to God, not to any human authority. Spiritual leaders now, as then, can keep the people in their direction for themselves, rather than directing them to God. St Paul was aware of this danger. 'I planted,' he told the Christians at Corinth, 'Apollos watered, but God gave the growth' (1 Cor. 3.6). In Corinth it seems to have been the people themselves who clung to their favourite apostles in an unhealthy way which split them into factions. Spiritual direction ought never to be allowed to become this kind of dependence-creating relationship. I may need fairly firm direction at one stage or other of my life, and I may need to trust the guide to know what he is about, without asking too many questions. But I remain personally responsible before God for following God's own guidance and growing in his grace. I am entitled to try and search out a competent guide. I am not justified in hankering after a spiritual guru who will save me from the pain of making my own decisions.

If opening a door and growing a plant are images of spiritual life, 'eading and following are metaphors belonging to a third image: the journey to God. Each of these images emphasizes part of the truth. Each needs to be set alongside the others. The journey image is found frequently in the Old Testament. The Israelites remembered the journey of Abraham, the wandering of Jacob, and the long trek of the whole people from Egypt as a model for their own journey of faith. They saw themselves as God's flock on this journey, with God as the shepherd of his people and their human leaders as shepherds under him. Priests and kings might be good or bad shepherds. Ezekiel rounded on the leaders of his day as worthless shepherds who used the flock only for their own selfish ends. He looked forward to the time when God himself would, as he had promised, be the true shepherd of his people (Ezek. 34). The New Testament also warns against thieves and wolves, and presents Jesus as the model of what a good shepherd should be (John 10, 1 Pet. 5.4, Heb. 13.20). Jesus does not manipulate or play power games; he does not take advantage of people's weakness and trust; he does not trample all over their beginnings of faith with hobnailed boots. He is a good shepherd because he is wholly open to the Father. He does not have his own hidden agenda. Other people may do any or all of these things. When they do they cease to help others to God and may indeed lead them astray. When this happens the sheep have to manage by themselves. No direction at all is sometimes better than bad direction.

This is one good reason for seeking direction in the context of a retreat. The person giving the retreat is limited to choosing appropriate passages of Scripture for meditation and perhaps giving some suggestions about growing in prayer. He or she is never working alone but is part of a team. There are built-in checks and balances in the process of a retreat. I thought I could be reasonably certain that people who give retreats in established Jesuit retreat houses are competent to do so. More important, in a retreat the director represents the whole company of Christian people. He is a sign not only that I am not alone, but also that Jesus is present as he promised whenever two people meet in his name. A directed retreat is much more than a time set aside to discover myself, or even to become more open to God, although it is an opportunity to do both. In a retreat I enter into a three-way relationship between myself and the retreat-giver and between both of us and God. I have to trust the person giving the retreat to be open with me and with God; I have to be open with God and the director. I have to believe that the director will lead me to God rather than apply his own programme for improving me. If I can wholeheartedly do this I can accept what I am given as coming from God himself and trust that Jesus is meeting me even when I do not understand everything that is going on.

Could I do this, I wondered, the first evening after supper, when the retreat began. The conventional illustration of faith loomed up again from my childhood. I had done my best to check the boat. I had prayed for guidance, and a whole series of indications had pointed me here. I now had to get into the boat and cast off the mooring. Did the helmsman know what he was doing? My reason told me that he probably did. My imagination was far from convinced. Dealing with imagination was the first thing that had to be done.

3 · Imagination

The Lord searches all hearts . . . (1 CHRON. 28.9)

God speaks to me through my imagination; he can't speak to me in any other way. Imagination is the faculty which sorts out all my impressions from the world around me, interprets them by means of what is already stored in it, and presents me with mental pictures, words, feelings and intuitive understanding of what is going on. A computer is in fact a good analogy: there is a memory – long-term and short-term; there is software which gives instructions for processing data; there is a printer or a display screen which presents information in a readable form. Input can be received either directly or indirectly; and there are computer hackers and 'viruses' too: human and other forces which can play havoc with our data and programming.

God's activity is itself of course independent of my imagination because it is spiritual. But my imagination is the only faculty I possess through which I can be made aware of it. My imagination receives data through my eyes and ears and other senses; it can also receive direct impressions from God, other people and all sorts of other sources. Some people are more sensitive to this than others, but everyone uses imagination all the time even if they do not consider themselves imaginative. Imagination is what enables human beings to interpret the world around them and respond to it. All human beings use imagination in order to make plans for the future and carry them out.

This is why using imagination in prayer is important if I am to respond to God in my daily life.[1] But not everything in my imagination comes from God. It is crammed full of all sorts of ideas, impressions and images that have nothing to do with God, or with how he made me, or with what he wants me to be. My imagination can throw up a host of false images to deceive me or alternative voices to command me; and my feelings and intuitions are equally unreliable as guides. This is why many Christians have opted to ignore imagination in their prayer and in their spiritual growth. But this means that they cannot use their imaginations safely at all. It may be possible to live without using imagination if you are a hermit or live in a community where every action is regulated down to the last detail. But it would be quite wrong not to use it if you meet with other people and make decisions in the world every day. Ordinary Christians who live and work among people who do not share their values and beliefs do have to use their imaginations in their daily lives. They therefore need to bring imagination into their prayer, so that God can cleanse it and enlighten it. And they need discernment to tell what comes from God and what does not.

Jesus promises his disciples that guidance will be given and that it is possible to follow it. He is the Shepherd whose sheep can hear and follow (John 10.3); he is the door to the one true security from falsehood (John 10.7). He is the true way to the Father (John 14.6); his Spirit gives the gift of discerning his voice among all the false voices of imagination (cf. John 15.26, 16.13f.). But the true gift of discernment is not an academic analysis of the babble in my head. A cacophony of sound rises to the surface of my consciousness just as soon as I stop talking. God's voice may indeed come to me in this form, as one among many other voices, each of which needs to be unscrambled from the interference from other signals, decoded and translated, like a coded radio message in a foreign language. But even if I have been able to decode the messages to hear what each of them is saying, I have no means of my own to tell where each comes from. This is what St Paul told the Corinthians, who were rather too prone to seeing every voice and impulse of their imaginations as a sign of God's leading, and even when their imaginations presented the babble in its raw, scrambled form they expressed it as the voice of the Holy Spirit among them. 'When you were heathen, you were led astray to dumb idols, however you may have been moved,' St Paul wrote to them (1 Cor. 12.2). The Corinthians were still liable to make mistakes about their inner promptings because they were full of pride and vanity, thinking themselves spiritually mature and possessed of heavenly wisdom when they were nothing of the sort. My own pride and vanity can lead me into the same errors, and St Paul's words to them apply to me as well.

There is *no* foolproof technique for discerning the Shepherd's voice. The only way to know where my true impulses are leading is to *look at the Shepherd*. If the impulses arising from my imagination lead me to dumb idols, then they are not from God but from the unregenerate pagan within. If they lead me to Jesus they are holy, because Jesus is the true image of God, and in him God's Word is made flesh in the world of daily experience. Reason is incompetent to deal with the irrational chaos below the surface of my mind. Raw, scrambled imagination can only be given form by images. If it is to guide me truly it needs to be formed by the image of Christ and not by the other images which are presented by the world as models for my life.

It is possible to develop discernment because I can choose to be governed by the image of Jesus. Connoisseurs of antiques and art develop an instinctive feel for the genuine not by studying techniques of forgery, but by immersing themselves in what is good and true. If my imagination is not to lead me astray, I need to do the same. It might be convenient if I could wait until I was truly poor in spirit before I made any decisions, but life does not wait for me to grow in grace. I grow in grace through my daily experience, not in spite of it. Opting out is not a practical possibility. But it is comforting to remember that the disciples Jesus called at first were not poor in spirit either. He taught them as they followed him and shared his life and listened to his words and went out to do his work. The *Spiritual Exercises* are designed to help disciples of Jesus who live in the world and are called to do his work in it to develop an instinctive sense of the genuine article; the same instinct that enables art dealers to make their fortunes. By immersing themselves in the truth of God revealed in Jesus, disciples today can learn the same lessons that the first disciples learned, and make true decisions even when they are surrounded with the world's values. But before they can even see Jesus clearly, God's people have to be set free from their idols and purified by submitting to truth. All of this goes on in a retreat. St Ignatius provides the conditions under which people's imaginations can be converted to the truth of the gospel.

I want to stress that it is only God who can truly convert a person's imagination. No human being has the right to re-programme another's mind. My imagination is converted when I turn from idols to serve the living God, whether the idols are painted statues in pagan temples or deep-seated images within my own unconscious mind. I do not need to make a pot-holing trip to my own inner caves in order to be converted. All that I can or ought to do is to offer my whole mind to God and let him deal with it as he wants. This is simply a matter of being faithful to the first Commandment to love God with all my heart and mind and soul and strength. The ordinary way that God deals with his people's imagination is by their ordinary daily habit of Bible reading, reflecting on what is read, letting it soak into the deeper layers of their mind (to what the Bible calls the 'heart') and then bringing more of themselves to God in prayer. 'Lectio Divina' is what the Christian monastic tradition calls this process, and Ignatian 'meditation' and 'contemplation' correspond to the reflecting and soaking parts of it, adapted for people who live and work in the world. Ignatius, like others who helped lay people to pray during the late medieval period, encouraged the use of imagination to bring the Scriptures alive. That is why Ignatian meditation is often wrongly supposed to be a question of letting imagination run wild. But imagination is not necessarily conscious in its operation. A person may have an active imagination which produces vivid pictures; he may be aware of God speaking to him in the form of imaginative pictures or words; or he may not. This does not matter at all. The end of the process, in whatever form a person is aware of it, or even if he is not aware of it, is simply being before God in prayer. Everything else is a means to that end.

I need help in order to begin the process of bringing my imagination to God in prayer. The director of an individually given retreat is a very important part of this process. By selecting key passages of Scripture and by the suggestions he gives, the director reminds the person making the retreat of the whole truth believed by the whole Church down the ages. My imagination is limited by what I have already experienced myself and what other people have told me. But the whole truth of God speaking to his people is much greater than the limits of my imagination. The director can help me go beyond myself and respond to God in a new way. The problem is that my imagination is already programmed against trusting anybody else to help me to God.

God's love is brought to me first by other people and, however wise and loving they are, they are human and make mistakes and give false impressions. Sometimes religious language is a shorthand way of referring to experience which a group of people share but which is difficult to describe accurately. People outside the tradition of the group may find this baffling. Children and others who have a limited experience to draw on may need help to fill in the outline provided by conventional language about God, in order to relate what is told them to their own experience. And they need to be encouraged to recognize and name the truth of God which they know for themselves. Concentrating on *religious* experience may in fact hinder rather than help them to do this. 'Religious experience' is one part of my whole experience of life. My conscious experience of God helps me to recognize and trust his presence and activity in the rest of my life, even when my feelings might lead me to doubt it. But before I was consciously aware of God's presence I was aware of images and ideas, feelings and activities, stories and poems, advice and rules; and all of this helped me to interpret my living experience of myself, my family, my friends and the world around me. Spiritual growth is growth in the ability to recognize God in all of it. But because it is also a growth away from self-centredness - including preoccupation with my own spiritual state - into genuine trust in God and love for him and other people, other people may see only the lack of 'religious experience' and fail to recognize the flickering spark in my life which is the beginning of faith and love. I can feel guilty for not coming up to their religious expectations. I can also be squashed when my own true experience is overlooked because I do not know how to describe it, or because my religious convention excludes it from notice. My own embryonic faith was so bound up with the conventional language of chapel tradition that it was not at all easy to tell which was which. Chapel tradition set great store by its ability to discern true 'saving faith' as the one valid criterion for baptism. But the result for me was the denial of my own faith.

This happened on the only occasion I ever responded to an appeal by going to the front. The preacher had asked those who wanted to give their lives to Jesus, or those who wanted to be baptized, to come forward. I had been trying to give my life to Jesus for years and I didn't particularly want to do it again that night, but I did want to be baptized. I had been asking my parents about it for over a year, and I'd even been to see the minister, but everyone had agreed that twelve years old was too young for real faith to have developed. The preacher, however, had said nothing about age, so I put my hymn-book down and walked forward, feeling terrified and determined and wildly hopeful all at once. A very kind lady from the congregation met me in the vestry. She gave me a card to sign which said: 'Today I Have Decided To Accept Jesus Christ As My Own Personal Saviour.' 'But I *haven't*,' I began to protest, and then stopped. What was the point of trying to explain? The lady wanted me to sign the card so that I could be baptized. I wanted to be baptized because I knew that was the beginning of Christian life and I desperately wanted to begin. So I signed the card but I felt bad about it for years afterwards. It seemed like getting in under false pretences. I knew that I had precious little of what anyone else in the congregation would recognize as 'saving faith'. But I also knew that I had to start somewhere.

Faith is not something you either have or do not have. It can develop from the smallest beginnings to something so strong and solid that it governs the whole of life. But its development is not a straight-line process; faith grows as it is stretched by circumstances and particular events that test it. These events may lead to growth or they may throw people off balance. During any of these periods of change my inner experience is just as chaotic as the jumble of impressions coming to me from my experience of the world around me. Before my faith has stretched far enough for me to be able to trust God in my circumstances and so come to recognize his leading, I am swung by my moods and ideas in many different directions, like a compass needle on a mountain with iron-bearing rocks. I can, however, choose to stay with the confusion or I can choose to follow the one attraction which leads to God, even if I am unable at present to tell which of my feelings represents my true desire for him. If I do not at least *want* to give my life to God, the painful process of detaching me from my own firm control of it cannot even begin. St Ignatius begins the *Spiritual Exercises* by stating the need for generosity (no. 5). He accepts a person's good intention as a valid starting point. I needed to start with the intention of offering myself to God at the beginning of the retreat, in order to come in the end to a point where I really could give him my whole freedom of will. That retreat led me further on from this first intention towards freedom from everything that hindered its fulfilment. Other people might not in the past have recognized my faith as such; I might have failed to recognize their genuine faith and love behind the conventional language they used; we might have denied each other's truth about God. That is why I have found it difficult to trust other people with my own deep experience of God unless I can trust them to accept my words for it. I have had just as much trouble with people who asked me whether I was 'baptized in the Spirit' or if I was 'a contemplative' as I ever did with people who asked me 'are you saved?' But what I *can* express to other people is my true, deep desire to give my life to God because there is no ambiguity in that. Being baptized was for me a way of stating my intention to die to sin and live the life of Jesus. Being confirmed was a way of asking for the power of the Holy Spirit in my working life. Making a retreat was similarly a way of stating my intention to bring my whole self to God in silence, so that his word could be spoken within me.

Making a statement of intent is not the same as describing an experience. I have sometimes mistakenly believed that it was. I have sung hymns of surrender to God so often that I have really believed that I have given him my life: 'Take my life ... take my silver and my gold ... take my intellect.' A retreat gives God the opportunity to show me that my experience has not yet caught up with my intention. He does not give me a comprehensive infra-red picture of the gaps and hot-spots in my world. He shows me the one thing necessary to bring me closer to him at this moment.

Making a statement of intent is a conscious decision to choose that one thing, whether I know it by a deep desire that draws me to God's love, or as a challenge to re-order my life in the light of the gospel of Jesus, or in the form of a command to carry out a task which only I can do, with the special gifts that the Holy Spirit will give me for it. Learning to recognize God's leading takes time and I need help while I am learning. My first experience of this attraction was a desire which I did not recognize for a long time as God's leading.

My parents had needs for beauty in worship which were not wholly satisfied by chapel tradition, and we used sometimes to attend an Anglican service when we went on holiday. I secretly hugged the memory of those occasional visits. I loved the candles and the stained-glass windows and the polished brass, and above all the feeling that there was something *there*. I recognized the same feeling, much more diffused, in the ordinary routine of school assemblies. The grammar school I attended had no formal links with any church, but the headmistress was an Anglican and sometimes used collects from the Book of Common Prayer. Her faith seemed to reflect out of those prayers which seemed so short compared to the extempore prayers of chapel, but solemn, like deep pools of truth. I liked the reverent way the Bible was read and the care we took to prepare the hymns we sang. I caught a glimpse of the same world again, later on, when I sang church music with the school choir and later again in a small choir at university.

It took me many years to recognize this obscure feeling as a sign of God's leading, because it was leading me in quite the opposite direction to the way I had been brought up to think that God led people. What about all those people, including my own father, whom God had led out of the formalism of their Anglican past to find freedom and true faith in the Baptist chapel? Could God really speak through the beauty of buildings and liturgy when my own tradition had chosen to renounce these things? My family thought that I was being beguiled by aesthetics and I wondered whether they might not be right. It needed more courage than I possessed to make the break with the Christian tradition in which I had grown up. But little by little I lost the sense of wonder and delight in choral music and church decoration. I still did appreciate them aesthetically but they no longer spoke to me of God. I had chosen not to follow that leading and something had died.

I had a favourite hymn about God's beauty calling to my spirit. I had a natural desire for beauty in worship which my parents shared, and I could have followed that desire. But I did not. The desire by itself was not enough to bring me to God. My own tradition was defective at the very point at which I needed help, because it failed to recognize that God *could* lead people to himself by means of this beauty. Within chapel tradition I could only interpret my own experience of God's gentle leading as false. Of course God did not leave me there; there were plenty of other stars to guide me to him and in the end I did find my way into the Anglican Church. But it was only after I had married an Anglican husband and made up my mind for myself to ask if I could be confirmed, that I found the mental framework of belief I needed to interpret my own experience as true. I was the only adult in a class of thirteen-year olds, but the Rector lent me books from his own library which opened up a whole new vision of Christian faith. Here was faith presented as something objective, something which remained the same whatever I thought about it. It was outside myself and it was solid; it was like a rock on which I could build my life, standing firm beneath my feeble grasp of it and supporting me in times of trouble. Faith began with what God had done, I discovered. It was not about my own subjective state of mind. Perhaps those who remained within chapel tradition had managed to come to the same conclusion without my struggles, but for me this was an enormous relief.

That experience of attraction, fear, doubt and certainty came back to mind as I looked at the psalms the director had given me to begin the retreat. 'Start this evening with the idea of praising God,' he had told me. The first psalm - Psalm 150 - reminded me that God is in himself worthy of praise. My imagination does not have the last word about him, because he is far beyond its power to comprehend. The true function of imagination is not to present alternatives to God's truth or his will for my life, but to give depth and variety to my response, like the full range of an orchestra. The second psalm – Psalm 139 – reminded me of what as a Christian I believe about myself. God made me from the beginning. He is with me in my darkest moments when I am not aware of him as well as at times when I have a strong sense of his loving presence with me. He created my deepest desires in order to draw me to himself, and he has his own plan for what he wants me to be. His will for me is built into my being from the time before I was born, but it may be opposed by all sorts of forces within me as well as in the world outside. 'O that thou wouldst slay the wicked, O God!' says the psalmist robustly. I had often felt uneasy about the bloodthirsty Old Testament passages calling down God's vengeance on his enemies, but chapel tradition had insisted that these parts of Scripture should be taken seriously as models of how to deal with whatever opposed God. The world was a battleground between his will and the wills of people and cultures and everything else that operated against him. I was a battleground myself.

The director, I realized, had given me a framework of faith in those psalms by which to interpret my experience, just as the Rector had done when I was confirmed. The perspective of those two psalms was to be the perspective from which I was to read my past life in the light of the Scriptures and understand what would happen over the next eight days. Making a statement of my own intention to seek God and his will for my life directed my imagination to God as he is, beyond the images of him contained in it. Accepting his perspective as the true one grounded my own experience in the reality of his goodness and love, and his good and loving purpose for my life. Only when my imagination is earthed like this can it receive true experience of God.

I had known that, too, I thought, as I looked back over the course of my life since I had discovered that 'The Faith' preceded *my* faith. It was at a parish weekend that an Anglican bishop solved my lifelong problem with the latter. He pointed out that Peter's declaration of faith in Mark 8.29 occurs at the mid-point of St Mark's Gospel. You don't need *that* kind of faith, he told us, in order to start following Jesus. I decided then that I really could commit myself wholeheartedly to being a disciple. I went home after the weekend and read straight through St Mark's Gospel at one sitting. The text, in a new translation, came to life in my imagination and challenged me with all its truth and mystery. The strangeness of the gospel confronted my own ideas about my life. As I finished reading my imagination presented a vivid picture of Jesus on the cross, almost as if he were really there in the room outside of my mind and I were standing in front of him. I knew, although the picture did not move or speak, that Jesus was asking me a question to which my answer could only be 'yes'.

That encounter had been a turning point, as the image of the crucified Lord challenged the false images which had been dictating the course of my daily life. Our small son was one of those babies who demand constant attention, crying through the day and night until he was about six months old. My image of myself as an outgoing young professional, able to juggle career and family commitments, flaked under the storm. The image of the smiling housewife gloating over her handiwork on the TV commercials pointed up my own domestic inadequacy. Inherited pictures of contented motherhood faded as my infant's weight chart drew the combined scorn of district nurse and doctor at the weekly clinic. As I sat through the weary hours trying to persuade my reluctant offspring to swallow one more spoonful of supplementary feed, the image of Jesus superimposed itself on society's images of success and strengthened my resolve not to give up.

The image of Jesus had modified my ideas of God's 'call' as well. This had been a recurrent theme of the visiting preachers and missionary speakers at my childhood church. 'Is God calling *you*?' they would thunder, fixing us with the penetrating gaze of a Lord Kitchener recruitment poster and sending guilty shivers down my back. I hoped fervently that God was not calling me. The things he called people to do for him appeared to be unremittingly nasty, and to require a degree of heroism I knew I did not possess. Nevertheless, I knew that one had to be willing to go anywhere for God if he *did* call. My Sunday School teacher had told me what happened to people who disobeyed the voice of God's calling. They ended up inside a whale, like Jonah. So when one visiting missionary issued a variant of the challenge I knew that the answer had to be 'yes'. '*If* God called you, would you be willing to go?' he had asked. We were supposed to be praying with our eyes shut, so that only God would see the raised hands of those who were willing to respond. But I could not resist the temptation to sneak a look around. To my amazement I could only see one other hand up. Its owner ended up in Uganda; I ended up in Tanzania. The rest of the congregation did not, to my certain knowledge, end up inside whales.

'I am the good shepherd; I know my own and they know me.' The image of Jesus as the shepherd who calls his sheep in a way they can recognize corrected my Lord Kitchener image of God and helped me realize that the fear of whales was an inadequate reason for obeying him, even if it had helped me to respond in the beginning. Jesus knows me: he knows exactly what I am like and what, by his grace, I am capable of becoming, and he continually calls me out of the security of the sheepfold to follow him. Being 'inside a whale' described very well my own experience after I'd rejected God's leading in childhood and adolescence; that experience helped me to understand what the book of Jonah was really all about. But the idea that it was possible to receive a special call from God in order to work for his Kingdom as only I could do never wholly disappeared from the background of my mind, even if my training as an architect and the course of my life hardly seemed to fit me for the kind of work conventionally thought of as 'full-time Christian service'.

Rob and I decided that our 'full-time Christian service' would have to start where we were. We began to look at our professional work in the light of the gospel which we had both encountered anew. Jesus was concerned about the people whom the society of his day despised. We began to look again at the architectural jobs we despised: the small-scale domestic conversions and the ugly little workshop extensions. In the light of the gospel they became opportunities to extend a professional service to ordinary people, rather than unprofitable commissions which stunted our own development as architects. It was a natural progression from this to offer for service overseas when the Secretary of the Church Missionary Society came to preach at our parish church and mentioned the need for qualified professionals to work with the

Anglican Church in other parts of the world. The Society had never to his knowledge been asked for architects, but after a long-drawn-out process of interviews, selection and training we had gone to Tanzania to work on a joint Church-Government project to advise and help people who wanted to build their own houses. We had been there for eight years, with home leaves in between tours of service. But now we were home for good.

God's leading in the past had been clear, I thought, looking back. But now it didn't seem clear at all. It had certainly seemed right to return as we thought and prayed about our decision and discussed it with other people. Conditions in Tanzania and in Britain had changed over the eight years. There were now local professionals as well as other expatriates to carry on the work we had begun. Government grant support for schooling in Britain had been abolished, and it was costing the Society more in school fees for our growing children than it had previously cost to support the whole family, despite generous private grants. My husband's elderly relatives were growing frail and he had no brothers or sisters to support them. The decision to come back to Britain had been the ordinary change of plans to account for changing circumstances which most people have to make at some time or other in their lives. But I couldn't help feeling a sense of anti-climax. Being a 'mission partner' had meant that I was serving God in a publicly recognized way. Back in Britain I was an ordinary member of an ordinary Sunday congregation and what I did from Monday to Saturday each week seemed to be no concern of the Church. Could I still know God's guidance as I had when we'd had 'professional' Christian status and the support of many other Christians praying for us? And what sort of guidance was I to expect?

My first feeling when I began to quieten down the daily concerns which normally occupy my mind was the feeling of being a stranger in my own country. When we returned, I had felt rather like Rip Van Winkle emerging from his long sleep to find that the world had changed in the meantime. I'd missed eight years of British culture. Even the vocabulary was different. The only desire I could identify with any certainty at the moment was the wish to settle back as soon as possible into normal society. But what was 'normal society'? Living in Tanzania had changed the way I looked at things and I no longer fitted in easily. Being a stranger in a Roman Catholic retreat house brought the same sense of strangeness into focus. I was in circumstances I no longer knew how to control. 'I don't fit in any more easily here,' I thought. There were cultural symbols of Catholic faith all over the house. 'Culture shock' was the name people at CMS gave to this feeling. It's what people are prepared for when they go to live in a foreign country, but I was less prepared for the reverse effect when we returned, although I had been told that it would happen. Culture shock is the effect on an imagination formed in one culture of encountering the symbols and values of another culture which is foreign and not wholly understood. It is a problem because it gives people a sense of not belonging anywhere and not being able to take part in life. Culture shock is the realization that you are powerless in someone else's society.

Culture shock is what happens in a retreat. The shock is caused not by the difference between Protestant and Catholic traditions and life-styles, but by the difference between me as I am, formed by all my past experience, and God as he is. God has his own purpose for my life, and it is good because he is good. But my own images of good and my society's images of success provide me with alternative models for my life. The feeling of strangeness - of restlessness and rootlessness - may be the sign of his love drawing me to himself, which I do not recognize as his love because my false images are stronger than the image of God within my imagination.

Golden calves are very easily recognized in children's picture Bibles and books on ancient art. One might wonder why the Israelites should be fooled into worshipping one when they'd been told quite plainly not to. The reality of golden calves is of course nothing like as straightforward as the pictures suggest. The values of the society in which I live are unreliable guides to God's truth, but the visible symbols of those values meet me every time I walk through a town, open a newspaper, switch on a television set, or buy the weekend groceries. They have an effect on what we all think of as 'good'. And what I think of as good may not in fact be at all good when it is judged by the whole truth which is found in God. Even if I have made a sincere statement of intention to love and serve God, and have directed my imagination towards his will for my life, I can still hide from his true call to me or reject it because the golden calves of convention lead me to make my life conform to a Christian model of success which is as false as the more obviously false images of the world around me. My imagination does not only need to be directed; it needs to be *converted*. Otherwise, every statement of intent I make will end either in disillusionment or hypocrisy.

Praising God is the first step in the process of converting my imagination. The director had given me the psalms to ponder in order to give me the wider perspective of God's vision of his world. But he had also told me to begin by praising God. I was not meant to leave my meditation at the intellectual or even at the imaginative level; I was meant to let it lead me to God himself in prayer. I could not praise God for what I did not believe was good. But I could *choose* not to let my imagination dictate to me what was good. I could praise God myself by using the words of the psalms I'd been given, and turning them into prayer. God *is* good, whatever my society says about 'good'. He *is* with me, even when my inner world tells me 'this is bad'. How was I to praise him now? Not, I decided, by ignoring the reality of my life and trying to salvage bits of my experience that I could count as success - *my* success - to present to him. The redemption for which Israel praised God in the psalms was *his* activity in their life, not their own. The psalms I'd been given lifted my imagination from the restricted boundaries of my own vision, and set it alight with a vision of the goodness and love of God. I might not see him clearly, but I did believe that he had led me here and that he was with me now.

I flicked through the examples of praise in the book of Revelation - a book surprisingly full of praise for one so devoted to cosmic visions of doom and judgement. I wondered whether the author wasn't going through a similar process of the imagination to the one I'd begun to engage on. He was painting images in words: seeing what was really good and true on earth when it was viewed in the light of eternity. His visions set the events which had sent him into exile on a remote island in their true perspective as part of a great process which would result in the triumph of God's love over all the forces of evil which opposed him. I couldn't yet see my life in that light, but I hoped that this retreat might somehow help me to do so.

In the rest of the book, I shall try to describe how it did.

Note

1. The question of using imagination in prayer is discussed with reference to the teaching of St John of the Cross by Ruth Burrows in *Ascent To Love* (Darton, Longman and Todd, 1987).

4 · The First Day

The beginning of the gospel of Jesus Christ (MARK 1.1)

The Gospel writers take nothing for granted. Each Gospel begins by linking the story of Jesus with what went before it: the history of God's dealings with his people, the interpretation of that history by the prophets, the history of all mankind, and the history of the whole creation. The gospel is embedded in a particular course of events, and all the preceding stages of history point forward in their own way to Jesus Christ.

St Ignatius takes nothing for granted either. What happens in retreat, when I encounter the gospel anew, must link back to my past life and point forward to the future. The *Spiritual Exercises* have one single aim. My director suggested that I might like to consider my own life in relation to this aim, set out at the beginning of the *Exercises* as the 'First Principle and Foundation'. He gave me the relevant extract in full: Man is created to praise, reverence and serve God our Lord and thereby to save his soul. The other things on the face of the earth are created for man to help him in attaining the end for which he was created ... Our one desire and choice should be what is more conducive to the end for which we are created (no. 23). We should, he said, use created things if they help towards that end and rid ourselves of them if they do not. I had already decided that there was no point in embarking on a retreat if I couldn't trust the director to lead me to God, but I had to admit that this passage set my Protestant nerve-ends tingling. Where was the gospel of Jesus Christ in that? Didn't it imply I could tinker around with my life in order to achieve salvation by myself? All evangelicals know that Christians are justified by faith in Jesus and not by anything they do. Was this director going to take an axe to the central pillar of my Christian faith?

He must have had an uncanny knack of seeing beneath the surface of my polite acquiescence to the deep-seated suspicions which lay below, because he looked me straight in the eye and told me that there had to be trust between a retreat-giver and a retreatant. I knew then that I'd have to tackle an area in my life that I preferred to avoid. I could not deny that I was wary not only of my fellow Christians but also of other Christians' points of view. I also knew why I found it difficult to trust them and this was not only a question of my own experience of God being ignored or squashed. It was more fundamental than that. The Christian Church is entrusted with the gospel of Jesus Christ. This is good news for all mankind. But different Christians have different views about what constitutes 'good news'. There are many different versions of the gospel, each with its own message of freedom and healing. And not all of them have seemed to me to be true to the Gospels' record of Jesus, even if they claimed to be based on the New Testament. Some people's 'Christ of faith' didn't have all that much connection with the Jesus described by Matthew, Mark, Luke and John. You can't dissociate serious study from your devotional life; what you believe affects the way you pray. And different Christian groups and traditions do have different ways of understanding the Christian message.

Chapel tradition had presented Christ as the Saviour of the World. I still believed that was true. But what does it mean to be saved? Some people who gave their testimonies had such resoundingly ungodly pasts to be saved from that I often wished my own life had been less respectable and ordinary, so that I too could know so certainly that I was saved. I'd settled for baptism and belonging to a Christian community which shared a corporate certainty of salvation in the future: we knew we *were* saved and therefore we would go to be with the Lord when we died. We were, however, a lot less sure about people from other Christian traditions. One of the reasons I took so long to become an Anglican was that I didn't want to trade the certainty of the faith I had in the Baptist denomination for the uncertainties of what was seen as Anglican woolliness. But was my faith in Jesus or was it in my own spiritual status? The challenge came when I was confronted by the hard facts of human existence which did not fit my conventional picture of 'salvation' at all.

41

In my final years as a student I had lived in a flat on the edge of the city's red-light district. My flat-mates and I all took the kerb-crawlers as a huge joke as we compared tallies for the number of cars which slowed down for each of us by mistake as we walked home from the bus-stop. We listened with glee as the landlady recounted the serial drama of our next-door neighbour's battle with vice; he would periodically sally forth with his knobkerry to purge the Corporation shrubbery in front of our terrace. But one evening it ceased to be a joke. I was walking home from the bus-stop when one of the girls on the pavement opposite caught my eye. She had thick pancake makeup plastered over her face, and her dead black eyes looked across the road at me. She couldn't have been older than thirteen or fourteen, and I'd never seen anyone looking so lost. It shook my conventional, respectable belief to the core. Jesus saved from sin: but whose sin was it that sold a child's body to men in well-pressed suits and shiny cars? I knew in my bones then that whatever the gospel meant it had to be good news for her or it wasn't good news at all.

That conviction forced me to question my own Christian orthodoxy. What was the 'faith' by which we were justified? How could someone like that girl possibly understand our well-drilled presentation of the gospel? I aired my doubts, only to be told that the answer was increased commitment and service. But was I committing myself to God or to Christian party propaganda? One of my friends was a Marxist and I wondered whether my own Christian belief was so very different from hers. Both Christians and Marxists aimed to convert people, train them in correct thinking, and send them out to convert others. Of course nobody could engineer the genuine encounters with Jesus experienced by many people, but I wasn't sure that our 'correct thinking' owed all that much to his inspiration. Didn't we, like the Marxists, operate a closed system, turning our backs on those we failed to convert and consigning them to the spiritual equivalent of a Siberian labour camp? Some of our talk about hell certainly seemed to point that way. There was never the slightest suspicion that any of *us* might ever find ourselves there.

That was the point at which I'd left the Christian certainties of my childhood behind and entered a twilight of half-belief shared for the first time in my life with those outside any church. It hadn't worked completely. I'd settled for a vague creed that kindness cures all, which had been quite inadequate to cope with the problems we encountered when we gave a home to a colleague at work who turned out to be an alcoholic and a confidence trickster, leaving a long trail of trouble behind him for us and for everyone we knew. I had wanted to find a true gospel which was good news for the outcasts of society whom Jesus himself had been concerned with in his own public ministry. But I couldn't find it without the help of the Holy Spirit, and the spirit of the tolerant sixties counter-culture was no more to be identified with the Spirit of Jesus than were the tight certainties of Christian convention. There was no good news in my own attempts to 'save' people; I needed to be saved myself from my incompetence to help anyone else. That was one of the reasons I'd made up my mind to find my way back to the Church. I knew I needed more than my own goodwill in order to live in the world. But when I did find my way back to faith, there could never again be any question of a closed circle of the 'saved' to which I belonged.

'Salvation' did not mean infallible certainty of my own spiritual status before God. But there were other interpretations of it which seemed hardly more true to the Gospels' picture of Jesus. Did 'salvation' mean material prosperity in this life? There had been close relatives who thought that we were foolish to waste our professional training on the work we started to do, converting dilapidated houses into flats for those who could not qualify for council housing. In those days that kind of work was done on a minimum budget and our fees were proportionately low. Some months we took a salary cut. Our relatives worried about the future we were providing for our children. They worried even more when we went to Tanzania. Weren't we being carried away by the spirit of liberal idealism? How could God possibly be calling us to the same pattern of life as volunteer workers who need not be Christian at all? We wondered whether the Holy Spirit could not work within the movements of thought in secular society, even if he was not to be identified with any of them.

When we arrived in Tanzania, we found that there were many other expectations about what 'salvation' meant. We knew we could not solve the economic problems of the Third World single-handed, but should we expect to convert it to Christianity? Did 'salvation' mean *Christian* success? It had certainly been exciting to be part of a great Christian missionary organization, but did that make us into Christian professionals, having to give evidence of God's work through us in order to justify the cost of sending us overseas? It was a temptation to tell a success story when we visited churches in Britain, leaving out the gaps and the loose ends and the human messiness which was so like Christian life in our own culture. But our life was not a success story. The reality of daily work in a Tanzanian Local Government office was far too like the work of an English New Town Corporation to project any glamorous picture of Christian development work. As for conversion, the only attempt at it had been made by a Muslim colleague who had spent the best part of a morning trying to persuade Rob that a religion which allowed him an extra wife or two would be a distinct advantage in his own domestic set-up, since his one wife was working outside the home. I'd sat in my corner of the office growing pink with embarrassment and wishing myself eleswhere. It rather put me off trying to convert anyone.

Could salvation be found within a Government office? Or did you have to work on a church-based project before you could claim to be engaged on 'God's Work'? I once sat in a prayer meeting saying 'amen' to other missionaries' fervent prayers for God's victory over the forces of evil which were opposing his plans, until it dawned on me that the plans in question had been refused building permission by my own husband. I hoped devoutly that no thunderbolt would strike him before I got back home. God's building plans had had very human executors, who had seen no need to comply with the merely earthly building regulations of a secular government and refused even to discuss the matter with its representatives, until the truth dawned on them too. St Paul would have known better: human authority is ordained by God in order to establish justice. But it was a temptation for *us* to see ourselves as a kind of 'justice ginger group' and forget that there were Christians working at all levels in the Government organization. Rob's opposite number in the Planning Department played the organ at the Roman Catholic cathedral. And there were plenty of other people who were working for righteousness and peace in society without being Christians at all; and there were Christians as well as others who seemed to be working against it, on the make for themselves or their own organization or group.

Some Christians were uneasy about thinking of 'justice' as part of 'God's Work' for this reason. They wanted to restrict the meaning of 'salvation' to God's work in individual people's lives and exclude his work in human society as a whole. But that didn't solve the problem of what salvation was. Religious people could impose crippling rules on each other in the name of freedom and faith, which were more restrictive than any secular laws of the land. Sin, lack of faith, lack of psychological integration, need for inner healing and poor self-image were all advanced as reasons for sickness and trouble, and for people's failure to recover the instant that they were prayed for or 'counselled' by well-meaning visitors. It had happened to me when I hurt my neck in an accident and took a long time to recover. Was that proof that I was far away from God? A 'stiff neck' was a biblical description of a stubborn heart. I knew quite well that I wasn't perfect, but did God really want to deal with all my inmost problems now? I was hardly in a fit state to let him; it was as much as I could manage simply to trust him for the strength I needed to live each day as it came. I developed a real sympathy with Job, whose 'comforters' gave him more or less the same message as mine had. Did 'salvation' really mean the kind of wholeness promised by the Power of Positive Thinking?

Even the spiritual battle with evil could give rise to different interpretations of matters of fact. One group prayed long and earnestly for an expatriate family who had been suffering from stomach trouble ever since their arrival. They identified the trouble as the direct work of the devil, and several attempts were made to deliver the patients from his clutches. When the family went home at the end of their contract, their more earthly-minded successors investigated the water-tank and found that the cover was broken and it was full of dead lizards. Does 'salvation' mean dividing

The Voice of this Calling

human life up into neat categories of 'good' and 'evil' and overcoming the latter by telling it loudly to go away? It didn' t matter so much when the demons were only dead lizards, but it did matter when family problems which ought to be resolved with love and mutual respect were subjected to 'exorcism'. I'd been involved in a situation like this, and it seemed as though my love and friendship had been rejected in favour of a fast-track, high-tech solution by a spiritual 'expert', just as Rob's low-level approach to building was often rejected by development 'experts' in favour of aid packages which promised instant results. We could both be hurt when what we were and what we offered in service was rejected; and it hurt even more when it was the Church, or Christians in it, who did the rejecting.

I'd come back to Britain with a well-developed distrust of my fellow Christians. I'd seen so many people do so much damage to each other in the name of Christ, despite a great deal of good work that was undoubtedly going on. How could I trust other people unless I could trust God to protect me from harm? He did not intervene to protect others from harm. How could I trust him even to meet me in the Scriptures, when Christians disagreed so violently about how the Scriptures should be read? For years I'd tried to relate the Bible to my daily life. Some Christians had thought that I was definitely unsound in my method of doing it. On the other hand, there had also been Christians who had classified me as the 'spiritual' and Rob as the 'unspiritual' partner in our marriage; they'd offered me alternative spiritual companionship. Rob, quite naturally, took a dim view of this. I could laugh about it with him, but how could I trust God to meet me in the Church when the Church was composed of such fallible human beings? I was absolutely determined not to trust *anyone* until they proved to be trustworthy. Not even Jesuit priests.

False gospels have false messiahs - false Christs - who save people from reality and deliver them up to a shadow world of make believe. One version of the false gospel detaches 'spiritual life' from ordinary life in the world. I'd been tempted myself to ignore the human weaknesses I shared with everyone else and to think of everything that went wrong as other people's problems. I could approach this retreat in the same frame of mind, treating my prayer as a dilettante exercise to create a fantasy world of escape from harsh reality: a week's holiday in a 'spiritual world' of my imagination. But the true gospel is not about escaping from ordinary life into a 'spiritual world'. It is about God's love for the real world, broken, sinful and unsuccessful and shot through with uncertainty and ambiguity. There are all sorts of spiritual currents in the world which influence me. But the Holy Spirit is the Spirit who bears witness that Jesus Christ has come *in the flesh*: as a full human being (1 John 4.2).

There had been other ways of escape which had tempted me in the past. Most people with fairly well-trained imaginations can succeed in visualizing themselves as they want to be. They may even be able to visualize other people as they would like *them* to be too. But these imaginary pictures are not necessarily what God wants, either for them or for their friends. My imagination is one of the things which can either help me towards the end for which I was created or hinder it. I needed consciously to hand it over to God for him to work in it and through it. Service of God is not imagining my idea of a perfect world and trying to make it happen. 'Thy Kingdom Come' means *God's* Kingdom, not mine. The Holy Spirit is the Spirit who leads me to acknowledge that Jesus is *Lord* (1 Cor. 12.3). It is his image which must be given form in the world, not the false images of human imagination distorted by sin. Jesus has to remould my own imagination and govern my entire life.

I began to understand that St Ignatius's 'First Principle and Foundation', which the director had given me as the background for the day's prayer, was, contrary to my first impression, the essential basis for the gospel. 'Man was created to praise, reverence, and serve God our Lord, and thereby to save his soul.' Jesus saves people from sin. He does not save them from their own diagnosis of what is wrong with them but from their basic orientation to 'praise, reverence, and serve' whatever is not God. False messiahs save me from their idea of sin, or my idea of sin, and instead of leading me back to God lead me further away. I had already begun to see how praising God lifts to the surface the closed areas of my life and the false images of 'good' as I acknowledge what is truly good. Reverence for God, I now saw, was equally essential. I needed to remember that I was his creature, lovingly made by him for his own purpose. I needed to respect the way he has chosen to order the world and recognize the mystery of his love for people, which I may experience but can never fathom. And before I could offer myself anew for God's service I had to recognize once again my own need of salvation. Otherwise I would simply be imposing my own ideas on other people. I had to know in the roots of my being that it is God who saves his world, not me. That meant learning once more to live by his Spirit and not let my unredeemed imagination govern my response.

Could I offer myself to God without any strings attached? I wasn't sure. There had been things which had held me back before. Even when we'd been packing up to go to Tanzania I had found it quite impossible to think of parting with a particular piece of furniture which I loved dearly. If anyone had asked me, I should have had to admit that I loved my Pembroke table more than I loved God. It had taken a long struggle before I was willing to let it go. In the end we had found a home for it and had not had to sell it after all. But that whole experience had made me realize that my commitment of my life to God was not nearly as thoroughgoing as I would have liked to think. I knew that I still clung to the good things of life.

'Inordinate attachments' are what Ignatius calls this kind of clinging. Inordinate attachments stop people seeing straight and making true decisions in accordance with God's will for them. Most of them are far more subtle and difficult to recognize than my attachment to my table had been. When we returned I had fewer possessions than before we went abroad. But I could still cling to my own ideas of making a good home for the children, getting re-established in work, being a good wife and mother. These things could sidetrack me into all sorts of inappropriate activities; I had to be honest about what was really necessary, not what would prove my worth to other people. And deciding on what was really necessary depended on knowing God's will for my life. If positive attachments could lead me away from that, negative fears could stop me wanting to find it. I knew I'd got to get rid of my fears.

The director had given me the story of Moses and the burning bush as the basis for my prayer; I was to read the story and then let it enter into my imagination so that I could, as it were, experience it from inside. He had suggested a prayer for 'a sense of the mystery and absolute reality of God' which, he told me firmly, is not destructive. I wondered if he knew how much I feared what might happen if I let God get too close. He also suggested that I should pray 'that I may know you'. I knew that I couldn't pray this prayer with Moses at the burning bush and *still* entertain fears about God's presence or his will for me, so I was looking forward to it. But when the time came I found it a tremendous struggle. It was as if I was looking at the biblical scene in my imagination through a thick pane of obscured glass. I could see the light of the burning bush flickering but there was no detail in the picture, and I couldn't get any closer to it. I tried to pray 'that I might know you', but the thought kept breaking in: 'You do know me. Now obey my calling.' I knew then that Moses' call was my call: to liberate God's people. I also knew that I was not going to get any further in prayer until I faced something I'd been pushing to the back of my mind for seven years.

We'd been in Tanzania just over a year when one night I'd woken up with the thought inside my head: 'Get a pen and write this down.' The whole household was asleep, so I fumbled in the dark for a torch and found a pen and some paper. 'This is what I am saying to you,' the thought continued. 'My church is in danger. I am sending you to build it up. Make straight what is crooked. Heal what is sick. And nourish what is faint from lack of food.' And then it stopped. My first reaction had been one of panic. I'd been brought up on the story of Samuel in the Temple hearing God in the middle of the night; but that story gave the impression that God's voice came from outside your head, not inside your imagination, and that you could hear it with your ordinary ears. Was this the same sort of thing or not? I'd heard of people in our own time hearing God's voice inside their heads, but they'd been a lot holier than I was. Was that *really* God speaking to me? Or was it me having delusions of grandeur? And if it was God, what did he

49

mean. 'Lord, you *know* my weakness,' I said to myself, only half praying to him. The thought came back at once: 'I know, and I have chosen you and sent you for this.'

Next day, after a restless night, I called on a friend I trusted and told her about it. Nothing quite like this had ever happened to me before, and I wasn't any more sure about it in the cold light of day than I had been last night. Could I trust it? I *thought* I'd had a sense of God's presence, I told my friend, but I didn't trust myself, not even about that. We both knew that I could get quite wild ideas of my own; and she knew as well as I did how easy it is to manufacture religious justification for what you want to do. But neither of us doubted that that sort of thing could and did happen to people and that it could be from God. It was just that I wasn't a very likely person for it to happen to. She advised against doing anything about it until it became clear what I *should* do. If it was from God, time and circumstances would confirm it. Meanwhile, it would be wisest to wait and see what happened in the world outside my imagination. As far as we could see, the Tanzanian Church was very healthy; it hardly seemed to be in any danger at all.

I took her advice but the inner thought wouldn't go away, even though I'd filed the piece of paper on which I'd written it down in a folder labelled 'Prayer: insights for future reference'. A few months later, when we were on holiday at the coast, I took some time away from the family to think by myself what it might mean. I hadn't told any of them about it. 'I'd know what it meant if it had happened to Rob, not me,' I thought, as I threw pebbles into the pools left by the coral and watched the ripples spread. 'But it said "you", not "him". So it can't be that.' I decided to make a start with what I *could* do. There were indications in our present circumstances which might be taken as confirmation. 'Build it up', for instance: I couldn't do anything about building up the Church spiritually, but all sorts of people including the diocesan authorities kept coming to us for advice on their building projects, and it was becoming quite hard to give them the attention they deserved while we were both fully committed to our own project. I decided to offer to take the load of the diocesan architectural work on our next tour. I couldn't do anything about the 'make straight' and 'feed' bits either; the Tanzanian church leaders were quite rightly cautious about letting anyone who came with a missionary society rush out to evangelize the local people or assume that their expatriate missionary status gave them the automatic right to preach and teach in church. That was a non-starter. But I'd prayed for the sick for a long time, and the parish group I'd belonged to in England had blossomed out into monthly healing services after I'd left, so perhaps I could do something about 'heal what is sick'. Obviously I couldn't do anything in church, but there was no reason why I shouldn't pray for people at home.

I *had* done that, I thought now. I *had* obeyed that call, as far as I could, and it certainly hadn't come to much. The diocese had files full of building projects, and I'd given all sorts of people lots of advice about their plans to build, but in the end only one two-room classroom block had actually been built under my supervision. That wasn't much to show for three years' work. And my attempts to 'heal what is sick' hadn't been any more successful. The hospital doctors and nurses healed dozens of people every week. I'd prayed with about half a dozen all told, until I thought I'd better let one of the church leaders know what I was doing, and he'd told me not to pray with anyone unless they specifically asked me to. The community at large was not exactly queuing up for my minis-trations. And after that I'd been sick myself with one thing after another until I was finally put completely out of action with the neck injury. When my neck had been bad I'd offered to prepare and lead some Bible studies as I did now have the time to do it. But the offer had been taken as a veiled criticism of those who saw themselves in authority within our group, and nothing but trouble had come of it. I still felt raw about that. I didn't want any more trouble. I'd tried to do what I could; but I couldn't and that was that. So much for voices in the night.

Now, as I remembered the things that had gone wrong and the struggles I'd had to find the truth of the gospel, I wondered if my natural wish to avoid trouble had led me onto the wrong track. There *was* error and sickness in the Church: I'd seen it with my own eyes. 'A bit of sound theology wouldn't come amiss,' I'd thought, and when my neck had immobilized me I'd begun to study a little.

But what use was that, here in England? I'd agreed with Rob that I'd do some of our final deputation preaching; but once that was over I could see no opening for any kind of 'official' ministry. Supposing – horrors! – God wanted me to *offer*? But to what? Last night at supper, I'd spoken to a bubbly lady who turned out to be an Anglican deacon from Wales. But the situation in England was quite different: it was at the time when there weren't any women deacons, because women deacons were seen as the thin end of the wedge. And the thick end of the wedge didn't even bear thinking about. It was all very well the director telling me I'd got to trust him, I thought, but how could I possibly tell him any of this? No self-respecting Jesuit retreat house would have any truck with ecclesiastical suffragettes. I prayed that if the Lord wanted me to mention it the director should raise the subject first. It seemed a fairly safe bet that he wouldn't.

I went down into the garden to try and sort out my confused thoughts. There was a life-sized stone statue of the Virgin Mary at the end of a grassy path, surrounded by trees. *She* did not make such a fuss, I thought. She knew what it was to be called to respond to God in a way that would put her outside her society's conventions. I walked down the path and stood looking at the statue. But Protestants have a deep-rooted suspicion of all Catholic piety concerning the Blessed Virgin. I had not realized how fundamentally I shared it until now. I wanted to talk to her, to ask for help; I wanted to understand what it meant to respond to God in a radical way. But I simply could not bring myself to address her. The yellow lichen curling over the head of the statue gave it a homely, familiar look. 'She was a human being like me,' I thought. 'And she made a totally appropriate response to God.' It started to rain. If I was going to do anything I'd have to do it now, before I got soaked. But I was *not* going to pray to a statue. There were limits. I turned my back on it, and addressed the air. 'Look,' I said, 'I need help.'

As I walked back to the house I suddenly knew that it would be all right, just as I'd known when I'd been able to stop clinging to my Pembroke table, nearly ten years before. Without realizing it I'd turned a corner. And just as I didn't in the end have to sell the table,

52

so I might never in fact have to enter the ordained ministry of the Church. I could let go of my own understanding of God's calling to to me if it turned out not to be what I thought it was. It had been my fear of it that had been blocking my response to God just as effectively as my attachment to my table had done. Fear was a negative attachment: not loving created things more than I loved God, but fearing their loss more than I trusted him to provide what I really needed.

I began to understand that reordering my life was not a superficial matter of rearranging my timetable, reassessing my priorities and, perhaps, making a few resolutions to carry out when I got home. I had the suspicion that it was going to entail a radical shift in my whole perspective: a major change in direction. This is what the Bible calls repentance. And this, of course, is where St Ignatius's First Principle and Foundation connects with the gospel. The beginning of the gospel of Jesus Christ is the call: 'Repent, because the Kingdom of God is at hand.'

5 · Tradition

In many and various ways God spoke of old to our fathers by the prophets (HEB. 1.1)

God had called me: I was not going to get a different call just because I happened to be making a retreat in a Jesuit retreat house. I had to work out what that call meant in terms of my own circumstances and the Christian tradition in which I was set. 'No,' I thought, ' "work out" is the wrong description.' What I had to do was to pray for light from God. 'Lord,' I prayed, 'I give you my life with all its goods. Teach me to reorder it according to your will.' If I could see my life in God's light, I thought, I could *be* like the burning bush: on fire with his love and not consumed because the fire came from him and does not destroy what he has made. What I hadn't realized was that the fire does destroy everything he has not made. You don't get set on fire with the love of God until the end of the process. I had to begin at the beginning.

During the retreat I said Morning and Evening Prayer from the Anglican Prayer Book. The psalm I read that day seemed appropriate:

> I will instruct you and teach you the way to go
> I will watch over you and be your adviser.
> Do not be like senseless horse and mule
> that need bit and bridle to curb their spirit
> (to let you get near them).
> (Ps. 32.8-9 JB)

There wasn't really much point in thinking I could be on fire with God's love when I was too frightened to let him get close. There had been an apocryphal story about a friend of ours we'd trained with in the School of Architecture: he had, it was said, an 'in' tray, an 'out' tray and a 'too hard' tray. I'd filed God's call to me in my own 'too hard' tray because I couldn't relate it to the rest of my life,

54

and all architects are uncomfortable when bits of their buildings don't relate to the rest. How could I build the Church when my own life didn't fit together properly? Perhaps I ought to look at that calling again. There were certainly things which needed straightening: there were as many false gospels around today as the fragments of false gospel the archaeologists had discovered from the first Christian centuries. And false teaching makes people ill: there were people suffering in all sorts of ways because they'd been fooled by plausible charlatans who came in the name of Christ. They needed healing and feeding with the true bread of life. God was calling me to make the truth known, and share what he had given me with others. *How* I did it was another matter.

What is the Church anyway, I wondered, as I waited for the director to come for our morning interview. Chapel tradition had proclaimed loud and clear the message that only those who had been baptized after making a public profession of their own personal faith in Christ were members of the true Church. This seemed to rule out nearly all Christians other than Baptists. Chapel tradition was harder on some other denominations than others, but I had found it difficult to believe that the people I saw each Sunday emerging from the Roman Catholic Church on the corner opposite our chapel were the enemies of the gospel that our preachers held them to be. The men wore the same sober suits as our ministers and deacons did; the ladies wore the same white hats and gloves. The message of our common culture was louder than the pulpit rhetoric. Had it been the same for them? Had their priests told them that we were dangerous heretics, and did they see us as fellow human beings despite what they were told? And was there really that much difference between the gospel as we proclaimed it and what they believed? The loud red and yellow poster on our notice board proclaimed 'Jesus Saves' to passers by; their life-sized pink plaster Jesus on his wooden cross showed how he did it. Both were crude, inartistic presentations of the gospel; but both were true. Like many people, I'd grown in ecumenical awareness over the years.

But ecumenical awareness didn't stop me seeing what was wrong in other people's versions of the gospel. I'd imbibed the doctrine of the priesthood of all believers with my mother's milk and it was in my bones, despite my present allegiance to the Anglican denomination. I couldn't see Anglican clergy as a race apart as some of my fellow Anglicans seemed to do; I'd been brought up to judge the truth of everything for myself, and I didn't see why I should wait for anyone else to make decisions on my behalf. That had certainly protected me from the wilder suggestions of spiritual mavericks. But it had its negative side too. I'd known I'd got to do something about this last night, when I was thinking about my attitude to people and things in my life. 'Attitude to People', I'd written in my notebook: '(a) stop judging them and repent of criticism; (b) forgive them and recognize my fault as well; (c) identify the error in thinking.' It all looked very pious set out like that. But I was still quite sure that I was right and they were wrong.

That was possibly why, when the director suggested that I should begin the second day of retreat with the story of the woman caught in adultery (John 8.1-11), I came up with my own plan of how to set about it. I would imagine all the people who had got things wrong, I thought, and I'd see them as the woman and see Jesus forgive them and then perhaps I should be able to forgive them myself. And I'd start by seeing myself as the woman, because I knew that I too needed forgiveness. I suppose, in the end, that this is what happened. But the meditation certainly didn't go anything like I'd planned. I came to the conclusion that trying to plan prayer is a mistake. If prayer really is a meeting with God I should not expect to be able to programme what will happen.

The day before I'd had difficulty using my imagination. It hadn't seemed to be working properly and only came up with the faintest outlines. But today it was quite different. My imagination took over completely and ran on by itself, without my being able to control it at all. I had intended to begin by imagining myself in the place of the woman, because I knew I needed forgiveness for getting things wrong just as much as everybody else did. But I had hardly finished reading the Gospel story when the scene came vividly to life in my imagination. The hot sun was beating down on a crowd of angry Pharisees confronting Jesus, who was sitting on a

56

low wall with the woman in front of him. And that woman was not me. There was no way I could change what was going on in my imagination; I simply could not be the woman. But I was in the scene. To my horror, I realized I was standing among the Pharisees, waiting for the signal to throw the rock which I held ready in my hand. And when the Lord said, 'Let the one without sin cast the first stone', I felt myself shutting my mind quite deliberately, and closing my hand round the rock; and then I threw it. Then everyone else threw theirs and the woman was lying on the ground with her head all smashed in. I thought, 'I did that', in quite a detached way, without any feeling at all, as if I were completely uninvolved myself in what I had done. Jesus just stood there. 'Perhaps he'll raise her to life again,' I thought. I knew he could make it all right again - but he didn't. He went on standing there, not moving, without saying anything. I wanted him to react to the situation and do something about it, so I called out, 'Aren't you going to say something? You are *my* Lord too.' But then something like an enormous steel shutter rolled down between me and everyone else, like the fire curtain in a cinema. It was quite dark and I was floating without any feeling or thought except, 'This is it. This is the outer darkness.' I don't think I'd ever really believed in hell before then. It wasn't at all like the traditional images of it: there were no flames and nothing was happening. I was completely alone in this dark void, and it was all quite final and awful.

'That's what happens when you judge other people,' I told myself shakily, as the solid shapes of the furniture and walls and window in my room reassured me that I was still in fact in the ordinary world. But what did it mean? It had been highly disturbing; not at all what I'd expected a retreat experience to be like. Meeting Jesus in prayer ought to be wonderful and uplifting; not like that. How could meeting Jesus mean being cut off from him if I believed the gospel and knew him as my Saviour? Perhaps I needed to see him as my Saviour now, I thought. I tried to imagine him dying on the cross for me, but my imagination was still not back under my conscious control. All I could picture in my mind was his hand, and I was using the stone I'd thrown to bash a nail into it as hard as I could. I realized that he was so identified with

57

sinful human beings that in judging other people I was judging him.

I'd prayed for the grace to be sorry for sin as the director had suggested, and now I certainly *was* sorry. But was that really a grace? It wasn't the usual way I thought of God's grace and its effects in my life. 'Must get this sorted out,' I wrote in my notebook as I tried to understand what the experience had meant. Was it prayer? Should I simply ignore it as the fevered product of an overactive imagination which ought not to be encouraged by making this kind of retreat? Was coming here a mistake? Eight days in silence was a very long time and I'd only just begun. Perhaps I was about to flip.

I felt thoroughly confused. I wasn't any more critical than other people I knew; I wasn't *really* like the Pharisees, surely? I believed in Jesus, unlike them. And I knew I was a sinner: it had been drummed into me from my youth up. But what had happened this morning had affected me much more deeply than I liked, even though I couldn't make any sense of it. It even affected my appetite. When I went down for lunch I found I couldn't eat anything. I forced myself to swallow a dry biscuit; it tasted like sand. What on earth was happening? I'd done quite enough praying to last the day, I decided, although I was not sure that *that* could be called praying. I'd scrub the rest of the meditations suggested. What I needed was to get out into the fresh air. A good long walk would put things back into perspective. I'd obviously overdone things this morning. I'd walk across the fields and get away from the house as far as I could.

It was a thundery day and the air was close and oppressive. I walked across the garden and out into a field where three horses were grazing, aiming for the hill further up where I hoped there might be a breeze. As I climbed across the field the horses came across towards me in inquisitive friendliness. And then, suddenly, the heavy atmosphere became charged with fear. The horses were not friendly; they were hostile. Even the gnarled hawthorns on the skyline were ominous signs that all nature was set against those outside the circle of God's protection. The world around me appeared as if through a distorting lens, and I began to realize what it must be like for a person in a close-knit pagan society to be cut off from his people by offending and thereby cut off from the unity of nature, so that instead of experiencing it as an all-embracing support in life, he finds it closing in on him in menace. I'd heard about that in Tanzania. In Europe it happens more often in the context of mental illness, but it is not only the expression of a sick mind. The Celts had known it well and had prayers which affirmed creation as one within the purpose of God, meditating his goodness and love. But they could only do that once they had known his salvation: when they had believed the good news of Jesus that had set them free from the curse of their old tradition. Apart from God, creation was not neutral. Human history was not neutral either. If I could not see God's work in creation and in human history as an act of his love, and share that love with others, then I put myself into the pagan way of seeing things, where nature is permeated with hostile forces and human history is meaningless.

The three horses stood in front of me facing me. This was no shift in perception or imaginary fantasy. It was real and I was frightened. I could not get past them. Whenever I tried to go round them, either to the right or to the left, the horse on the outside side-stepped to block my path. And then the horse in the middle took my coat sleeve in his mouth, gently but firmly turning me round. He walked me the two hundred yards or so back to the gate before letting go of my coat. The three horses stood shoulder to shoulder in the gateway as I walked slowly back to the house. 'I have a choice,' I thought. 'Either I can see creation apart from God: a place to run and hide in from him. But in that case, creation isn't creation: it becomes hostile nature. Or, I can see creation as united in God's purpose and a sign of his love for me. If I do that, the incident with the horses may be significant. Perhaps it means that God isn't going to let me run away from him any more.' It was like the old song about the Last Judgement: 'O sinner man, where ya gonna run to?' There wasn't anywhere to hide. And then the psalm I'd read in the morning came back to mind: 'I will instruct you and teach you the way you should go ... be not like a horse or a mule, without understanding, which must be curbed with bit and bridle' (Ps. 32 8-9). Those horses hadn't had bit or bridle, I thought, but perhaps they had been more responsive to God than I was.

I went back to my room and began to read the next passage from St John's Gospel which the director had given me for the day's prayer, John 8. 15-16. I could still picture myself as a Pharisee, so that Jesus seemed to be speaking directly to me. 'You judge according to the flesh, I judge no one. Yet even if I do judge, my judgement is true, for it is not I alone that judge, but I and he who sent me.' Jesus challenged my whole basis of judgement. Like the Pharisees I had been looking at people and events from a falsely human point of view which left God out of account. 'Spiritual' people were particularly prone to do this. The Pharisees were the spiritual élite of Israel in Jesus's time but they were passing judgements on other people from their own point of view – 'after the flesh'. That kind of spirituality increased people's power for evil not for good. The Pharisees had been given the keys to the Kingdom of Heaven, but they had used them to shut the door on themselves and everyone else. You could see yourself as specially chosen by God in a way that made life intolerable for other people.

Had I done this? I'd picked up Pierre Teilhard de Chardin's *Hymn of the Universe* (Fontana 1970) in the library and a passage on a page I'd opened at random had struck me; it described his struggles to accept that God was calling him to a way of prayer that he and everyone else feared was 'pantheism'. My fear was different but I understood exactly what he meant. I'd had a struggle earlier in my life to accept that God might be leading me into the Anglican Church. But after that I'd had another struggle and it was still going on. I couldn't even *tell* other people about the way of prayer that I thought God was leading me in. I'd tried, once or twice. Various people had done their best to find out. But when I began to mention it to either good charismatics or sound evangelicals they threw up their hands in horror and warned me darkly of danger. And I hadn't told them half of it. It might worry them but it worried me even more. I realized that I'd passed my own judgement on *that*, too. Once more I'd refused God's leading and landed inside a whale. And this time I had no idea how I was going to get out. But unless I was living close to God, praying in the way he wanted me to pray so that he could speak to me, I would carry on passing judgements on everything from my own point of view. My understanding of myself as specially called by him could then lead me into all kinds of error in his name.

It was tea-time but I still didn't feel hungry so I decided not to go down to the dining-room. I made myself a cup of tea in the kitchen at the end of the corridor and brought it back to my room. I wanted to carry on thinking about what was happening in my life, because all this did seem to be leading somewhere. I read the next passage in John 8. This time Jesus was talking to the people who had believed in him but who were bound up by their inherited tradition, so that they were not truly free. 'If you remain in my word you will indeed be my disciples', he had told them. 'You will learn the truth and the truth will make you free' (John 8. 31-2). 'Remain in my word . . .' What did it mean? Different translations shed no light: 'abide in my word'; 'make my word your home'. What did it mean to *live* in the word of Jesus? The first verses of St John's Gospel which I'd been thinking about the day before came back to mind. 'In the beginning was the Word, and the Word was with God and the Word was God. . . . all things were made by him, and without him was not anything made - - -' (John 1. 1, 3). 'If we live in *that*', I thought, 'we live in the living Word of God; the creative word of life.' That meant I could draw out the truth of things without having to pass judgement on what was inadequate or even on what was false: God could deal with that.

'Well,' I told the Lord, 'this week I will stay in your creative word and be made free by your truth.' I had the feeling that he was quietly killing the old Protestant in me. Perhaps that was no bad thing. The end results of judging are plain to see throughout the history of the Church: schism; inquisitions; complacent immobility. If it was a question of tradition versus God, tradition would have to go. My unconverted wish to make my own judgements was a deadly influence in my life, fighting against God's love for me and for other people. I began to understand the meaning of what I had seen in my imagination that morning. What appeared on the surface to be quite trivial faults were only the visible tips of huge icebergs: parts of my life which were frozen solid, impermeable and untouched by the grace of God. Wanting to be a Christian success was a symptom of a whole way of thinking that denied the truth of the gospel. If I really believed that Jesus is Lord I would not be so concerned about my own lack of success, nor so hasty in forming opinions about other people: I could leave both to him. Neither had ever before seemed to me as a particularly serious sin. But seen from this perspective they appeared as they really were: tendencies which led in the end to the kind of murderous hostility which would unthinkingly destroy all that stood in the way of what I judged to be 'good'. That was no way to begin to 'make straight what is crooked', I thought. It seemed that until now I had merely been playing with the notion of giving my life to God and obeying his call. I had made sure that I retained control over what was most important to me: my own power to judge for myself. I'd told myself that conversion was a lifelong process and I couldn't expect too much of myself all at once. But now I really did want to change. That was at least a beginning.

6 · Conversion to Christ

... but in these last days he has spoken to us by a Son ...
(HEB. 1.2)

How do you change the deep imagination which conditions the core of your personality? I believed the gospel with the surface of my mind. But underneath were deep images which had not been touched by its truth. My imagination contained the memory of Cain, the archetypal murderer; and St John's Gospel told me quite clearly that the source of murder is not God. 'Lord,' I prayed, 'crucify in me all that is not of you.' My choice was not between obeying or not obeying God's word; it was between being a child of God or a child of the Devil, the father of lies.

The director had told me that morning that chapter eight of St John's Gospel brings out the characteristics of the world's opposition to God. The source of that opposition was Satan, the murderer and liar. I'd met so many people who seemed to see devils round every corner that I'd rather dismissed the idea of any *personal* will behind what opposed God. But sin was more than human. My resistance to God took on a new, sinister significance. It wasn't merely a matter of resisting God's leading in prayer. Behind that resistance lay a deep false image, demonic in the true sense of the word. Operating in my imagination was a lie: an image of God which was false, presenting his true call to me as fearful and crippling, and eating away the fruit that it should bear so that it rotted from inside before it ever ripened. My life seemed to stretch out like a desert, back into the past and out into the future, brown and barren, without any hope of growth or fruitfulness. The dreary sins of disobedience and faithlessness unrolled themselves before my imagination: the small deceits and pretences as well as the niggling criticisms and judgements of other people. There was the inertia and resistance which had wasted all that time. There was the unbelief that still worried about the future and the fear which seemed to have me in its grip more firmly than ever.

I decided that the only thing to do was to stick to the suggestions for prayer that the director had given me in the morning. 'We can give the Lord our sins,' he had said. Now I wanted to do this. As I was thinking about it my imagination brought up a vivid picture of Jesus on the cross. Rather hesitantly I asked Jesus to take all the sins I'd seen in my life, and put them there. His reply took me by surprise:

'No,' he said. 'I will burn up these sins in you. You come up here on the cross.'

'We can't both be there,' I objected.

'I will be in you and look through your eyes.'

It was very odd. I had the same sense of detachment that I'd had in the morning, without any thought or feeling. I looked down. I could see his mother and St John, some other women and then the crowds of people, stretching out in every direction until they were blurred into the distant hills.

'They put you here,' said the Lord. 'Do you condemn them?'

'No, Lord, you don't condemn them,' I replied. I knew that.

'Do *you* condemn them?' he repeated. 'They put you here.' Suddenly I had a sense inside myself of his own endless compassion for sinners, and I knew that I really did not condemn anyone any more.

'Remember this,' he told me.

'Nothing that anyone ever did to me is anything like what they did to him,' I thought. 'No, not "they"; *we* did that to him. Nothing I think of as wrong with anyone else's belief or practice compares with the whole sin of the world which crucified Jesus.' I was part of the one world which had done that. I could forgive, too, by being one with his forgiving heart.

It was as if the dreadfully oppressive atmosphere of the day had lifted as my sinful life was brought into the light of the good news of God's love for the world. Even the weather had changed. The thunderclouds had vanished and the evening was clear and bright. I went for a walk down the road. Sunlight was streaming low across the valley, touching trees and fields with gold. 'The light of Christ in creation,' I thought. 'Not just creative, but redeeming and re-creative love.' People were working in their gardens, cars were passing on the road, tractors were ploughing late in the fields. Everything was bathed in the same golden light. I leaned over a field gate, letting the warmth of the sun soak into me.

'Do you condemn them?' he asked again.

'No, I don't condemn them.'

'Neither do I condemn you,' he said. 'Go in peace and sin no more.'

But what about all those who had got things quite wrong? It wasn't only *me* who had false images of God operating in my imagination; my false images came from outside myself as well. It seemed as if the Lord was reminding me again of all the times I had disobeyed him myself. 'If I turn away from the true light so often,' I thought, 'how can I condemn those who do not see it clearly?' But it was difficult not to. Even my most inward experience of God can be distorted by false images, misinterpreted and denied. This had affected my whole practice of prayer.

One of my first images of God had been the image of a high window, with the deep blue sky beyond 'that shows nothing and is nowhere and is endless'. But the whole tradition of the Hebrew and Christian Scriptures is that this unknown and unknowable God has in fact chosen to make himself known. He has not revealed himself to everyone but only to some, and not to the most worthy, respectable, devout or intelligent people at that. This is profoundly shocking both to human pride and to human sense. Adults can rebel against the scandal of it and prefer the 'nothing and nowhere' of Larkin's 'High Windows' as being more worthy of a transcendent God. And yet I *did* believe that God was drawing me into a form of prayer without words or images. Was that really God or was it my own pride? I could quite easily end up as one of the typical Christian casualties of this kind of prayer, thinking that I was God myself: my husband and children recognized the danger when I went 'spiritual' on them and steamrollered everybody else's opinion.

And then there was 'praying in the Spirit'. I'd been a member of a prayer group before we left England for Tanzania, and we'd prayed for sick people in the parish together, holding them up to God in silence. But I'd had difficulty praying at home for some people who were mentally sick, and when I was wondering how to pray my father had sent me a book in the post, quite unexpectedly, with a short note to say that he felt strongly that I ought to read it. I was intrigued and began to read it there and then, sitting on my unmade bed with the children playing on the floor beside me. I'd read three chapters about the author's new experience of the Holy Spirit which had brought him greatly increased joy and assurance in his Christian life and work. But what struck me most about his story was his account of a prayer without intelligible words which was different from the wordless prayer I knew. *That* was the answer to my wondering about how to pray for all those people suffering from mental disturbance, I had thought. I had not paused for reflection. I had got straight down on my knees and asked God to give me that gift of prayer too; and he had, as I knelt there with the children still half-dressed and the day's household chores waiting to be done. But I hadn't altogether agreed with the interpretation the book gave to that kind of prayer, when I read the rest of it some time later. It seemed to me that it was a way of allowing the Holy Spirit access to my own inner chaos, so that I could pray for those whose inner chaos had erupted out of control. I preferred what I'd been taught in my confirmation class to some of the teaching in the book about the Holy Spirit. Then there was all the difficulty I'd had both in England and later on in Tanzania with people who held out glittering promises of 'Pentecostal power', as if the experience of this prayer I'd had could turn me into a comic-book super-hero, calling for signs and wonders and zapping the opposition, human or demonic. As a result I hadn't been able to relate that way of prayer to the rest of my life with God.

There was prayer to Jesus too. I certainly had seen the image of Jesus as a challenge to my everyday life but even *that* could go wrong. I had rejected both the chapel slogans like 'Jesus Saves' and the crude images of him, particularly the images which reminded me of Holman Hunt's picture. Jesus was a *Jew*, I'd thought. When we'd been training to go abroad with the Church Missionary Society we had discussed our images of Jesus and how they were often really images of national heroes. I'd picked out the one picture of Jesus which did not have long blond curls and I'd never noticed that the figure carried a gun on its back. The image of the Saviour who brings justice to the nations was just as corruptible as the other images of God.

It was love that redeemed the world, I thought now. Without love all our prayer is misdirected. The high window really does show 'nothing'; the influence in our lives really is blind, like a cosmic wind of fate; and the Kingdom of God is brought in with force: guns, not forgiveness. Talk about God's 'power' is very ambiguous. God's love is beyond all imagining; but electricity is hard to imagine as well. And some of the books about prayer that I'd read did seem to stress the electricity image of God at the expense of the fatherly one. Even 'Catholic' prayer wasn't proof against this: you could think of prayer as an activity best carried out in convents and monasteries where it was safe to engage in it; you could see monks and nuns as a professional class of expert engineer, acquiring the technical knowledge they needed to tap into a high-voltage power current without getting sizzled up and, perhaps, transform the energy down to a low-voltage grid for domestic consumption.

That was what the golden calf had really been about. It was an image of God's footstool which gave the impression that God was *subhuman*, not *more* than human. It symbolized the natural energy within creation. God had called his people to a deeper knowledge of himself than this, and that false image led them away from him. Had it led me away from him too? What, after all, is distinctive about *Christian* prayer, apart from the love of God given to us in Jesus? There are plenty of contemplatives in other religious traditions, and there are three different ways of approaching this kind of prayer which were outlined by Plato, nearly four hundred years before Jesus was born. There are words of revelation in other religions too: people prophesied before Pentecost, and if not all the prophets were true, not all of them were false. And the great religions of the ancient East had all sorts of techniques for inducing imaginative dream-like fantasy visions: there is nothing specifically Christian about *that*, either.

God in his goodness hears prayer however it is made, if it is made

67

sincerely to him. He saves people who do not know him at all, as the prophets reminded Israel (see Amos 9.7, Zech. 9.7). But a god who can only be approached by experts with the right knowledge and techniques can never save anyone. Only the true God who out of sheer love comes down to act within human history and makes himself known to ordinary unskilled human beings can really save them. Golden-calf religion, and modern electricity-religion too, is a way of getting the world to work the way the experts think it ought to work. That is not salvation for anybody else, because they are doomed to a second-class existence, and what is good for the experts is not necessarily good for them. But it is not salvation for the experts either; if they fail to perform all their prayers and discipline properly and exercise the right kind of 'faith', the world will cease to function for their benefit. Golden-calf religion and electricity-religion are inspired by the spirit of fear, and it is not the true fear of the Lord from which wisdom springs. The root of true fear is reverence. The root of false fear is selfishness. That is the difference between true and false religion, and between true and false prayer, whether it calls itself Christian or not. I thought of my own prayer and my own fear. That wasn't true fear. And only perfect love casts out false fear: the love of Jesus. I had had a sense of his compassionate love today. I decided that I should like to pray tomorrow about having this compassionate heart of Christ within me.

The last prayer of the day was meant to bring everything that had happened into the light of God's redeeming love, summing it up in a conversation with the crucified Lord. I didn't quite know how to tackle this, because it seemed as if that was what had happened earlier on. But I looked at the text I'd noted down from the *Exercises*:

> Ask how it is that though he is the Creator, he has stooped to become man, and to pass from eternal life to death here in time, that thus he might die for our sins . . . As I behold Christ in this plight, nailed to the cross, I shall ponder upon what presents itself to my mind. (no. 53)

What actually presented itself to my mind before I'd had time even

68

to close the notebook was one of those cheap plaster Sacred Heart statues which are sold in the traditional kind of Roman Catholic shop. It was an image I'd always found tasteless. I did *not* want to ponder that. '*Spiritual Exercises* is a good name for this,' I thought. 'Hurdles today.' All I could feel was a tremendous anger: anger to the Lord for involving me in the bottom end of Catholic kitsch. I could imagine myself as one of the more violent Protestants at the Reformation, going round smashing up images. For the first time in my life I understood what had motivated them.

'Yet we do not smash the vessel from which we have drunk the wine'. The words of a half-remembered quotation flicked up from my memory as if they had just been spoken, and caught my anger in check. It was a line from chapter 58 of *The Cloud of Unknowing*, a book about prayer by an anonymous medieval author. The book's central theme is that God is beyond all images of him, but that there are right and wrong ways of going beyond images in one's own prayer. It was heretics, said the author, who smashed the cup of visible miracles and physical gestures and revelations given in bodily likeness. Revelations given in visible form are meant to help people understand a spiritual truth that they might never grasp if it were given in any other way. The little Sacred Heart statues were reminders of a revelation of this kind, given to various people from time to time over the centuries in the Western Church. The image of the Sacred Heart was a way of keeping alive the knowledge of God's compassionate love revealed in the humanity of Jesus, at a time when it was in danger of being forgotten amidst the speculations of the scholars.

Was I a heretic too? Why did I fell so strongly that I wanted nothing to do with that particular representation of the Lord? Was it really because of the external form of the image? Or was it because I couldn't accept the reality it represented? I'd long since given up any attempt to make sense of religious language about hearts. I didn't want to think about my heart; I didn't want to think about the heart of Jesus either. At least I didn't want to think about it like *that*, in a human form. I thought of the sunlight I'd seen streaming down the valley in the early evening. I could cope with that. That seemed a much better symbol of a love which does not

69

put people through emotional hoops to see if they are worth saving. I'd rejected too all the high-pressured appeals to my feelings made by preachers over the years; I didn't want a God like *that*. 'I don't want sacred hearts,' I decided. 'I want pure light streaming through the universe.' But I was beginning to understand that if I couldn't accept this, I should lose the light as well.

It seemed almost as if I were being offered another chance to accept the truth behind the forms I had rejected in childhood. I turned my attention back to the Lord. Suddenly I realized that his heart was the *source* of the light. It was the heart of compassion that I had felt before. He was offering me a deeper relationship with himself. And I had been refusing it. 'You can't be transfigured in this light,' he said, 'without having this heart within you.'

That heart was the one centre of the world's true light. That heart alone could bring the separate compartments of my own inner life together and unite it. And that heart was the only source of love strong enough to drive out my own fear. Jesus could burn up my deepest idols and convert the murderer within me. But I couldn't guess how it was going to happen.

7 · The Servant of the Lord

Now you are the body of Christ and individually members of it
(1 COR. 12.27)

The next day was Sunday and I decided to go to Mass in the chapel at the house rather than search for an Anglican church outside. The Anglican Book of Common Prayer talks about being 'in love and charity with your neighbours' as a condition for coming to Communion. Not only had I seen yesterday how far from 'love and charity' I was, but I was also beginning to realize that I was a member of a church which had not been 'in love and charity' with its Christian neighbours for four hundred and fifty years. I prayed before I went down to the chapel that I might know what our disunity means to the Lord. 'This also,' I thought, 'is a consequence of our judging each other.'

I'd been to Roman Catholic services before and I felt quite at home in the congregation among the lay people who came for the Sunday service. The liturgy was almost identical to the modern Anglican rite we'd used in Tanzania. We sat round in a semi-circle singing choruses to a guitar which was very slightly out of tune, just like the guitar played by one of the members of a prayer group I'd belonged to there. But all the way through the service, so very familiar in all its surface details, I was aware of the deep, deep rift that divided Protestants and Catholics. I knew more of our common history now than when I'd stood on the chapel steps and wondered what difference there was between us and the Roman Catholics over the road. I'd joined in Bible study groups with different denominations, and I knew that it could be quite difficult to tell the difference between denominations by what people said. I knew something about the efforts that theologians were making to overcome our doctrinal disagreements. But were we really any closer to unity? The shelves of the library here revealed a whole unified structure of belief and doctrine, built up on assumptions

71

about God and his grace which Protestants simply did not share.

A member of the Community gave the address. He spoke on the gospel for the day: the parable of the labourers who were all paid the same wage (Mt. 20. 1-16). As he described how we exclude each other by neglect as well as by passing judgement I felt the tears beginning to run down my cheeks. He could have been speaking directly to me. 'Yet we *are* one in Christ,' I thought as I took my neighbour's hand for the Peace. She looked a sensible, homely person, dressed in a tweed skirt and Aran sweater just like the countrywomen in the Mothers' Union at home. I should have liked the opportunity to get to know her. 'Peace be with you,' she said. 'And with you,' I replied. But then, as the congregation went forward for their Communion and I sat in my seat, the picture of the woman I'd seen yesterday flashed back to mind, quite vividly. Her face was the face of my neighbour. But when I looked again I saw that it was Jesus, stoned and battered by our judging each other, covered in blood and with his skull crushed. *That* was what our disunity means to him.

I couldn't stop crying. I hoped that the others wouldn't notice, but in a sense I was past caring what they thought. What mattered was not what they thought of me but what we all thought of each other. Somehow I had to break through to a true vision of the unity which is already ours in the peace of Christ: the love and the joy and the peace which transcend the wrong. There has always been wrong, inside the Church as well as outside it. Even the saints who were most insistent that all would be well in the end knew that. They were not shutting their eyes to the problems. They'd got through to a different level altogether.

Jesus didn't shut his eyes to the problems either, I thought. St John's Gospel describes how he prayed for the unity of his disciples *after* one of them had gone out to betray him, and when he knew that those who remained with him would be scattered and fail before the night was out (John 17). There must be more than the fact of human failure, or there is no point uncovering the depths of what is wrong. Jesus died to save us from sin: and that must mean the sin of division in the Church of which I am part as well as sin in general and the sin which I am aware of in myself. I had to begin to see our divisions in the light of his salvation; and only he could show me that. All I could see now was how much they hurt him and wounded his body. And yet I knew that it was his wounds which heal his people. How could this be?

At the end of the service, I remembered a poem by Gerard Manley Hopkins which seemed to speak of the renewal of the Church and the world in the unity which God intended:

> And though the last lights off the black west went
> Oh, morning at the brown brink eastward, springs –
> Because the Holy Ghost over the bent
> World broods with warm breast and with ah! bright wings.

There was hope of renewal because God is God the Creator and Redeemer and giver of new life to the dead. 'Sunday is the day of resurrection,' I thought. It seemed an appropriate day for the third day of retreat. I thought about renewal in the Church as I went back to my room after the service and reviewed yesterday's prayer in readiness for the director's visit. Renewal in the Church seemed to parallel my own experience of renewal. So many seeds of new life in so many places, and yet so often what started off well seemed to end in judgement and schism. Was it possible for the Church to be renewed *without* Christians passing judgement on who was 'renewed' and who was not? What *did* go wrong with renewal? There were just as many divisions thrown up as a result of judgements passed on other people's spiritual status and quality of Christian service in the twentieth century as there had been in the sixteenth. Some people thought the answer was to tighten up the Church's institutional authority and take a firm stand against those who fanned the flames of doctrinal debate or criticised hallowed traditions. Others thought that the only course was to come out of an institution that was hopelessly corrupt or rigid and form independent groups where the true voice of prophecy could be heard. But if the Holy Spirit was the Spirit who inspired institutional leaders *and* the prophets who spoke out against injustice and corruption in high places,[1] it hardly seemed possible to draw a line down the middle of the visible Church so that all the faithful, obedient Christians were on one side and all the apostates

73

and heretics on the other. There was indeed false teaching, and people did turn from the Lord as a result of accepting it. But it seemed to me that the battle went on equally fiercely everywhere between true and false worship and just and unjust conduct: in the Protestant and in the Catholic Church, in small groups and in the Establishment.

It wasn't always easy to tell what was the prompting of the Holy Spirit and what was not. That was perhaps why St Ignatius did not talk much about the Holy Spirit but only about 'good spirits' and 'the evil spirit'. If you made a mistake about the Holy Spirit you could find yourself unable to respond to God at all. It didn't make much difference whether you followed a false spirit thinking it was the inspiration of God, or whether you reacted against those who claimed to be inspired by the Holy Spirit by refusing to talk or even think about him because of what went wrong. Perhaps I'd done this, I thought now. I was afraid to speak out about what was wrong. I was afraid to trust even what seemed to be good inspirations and act on them, because I had seen so many good beginnings go wrong. If some of the things I'd seen were, as some people claimed, the work of the Holy Spirit, then I didn't want to have any more to do with him ever again. Did he really inspire Christians to judge each other and condemn each other and point out each other's inner hurts and weaknesses, without giving them either the power to overcome these things or the true teaching that would show up what was right and wrong? Was it really his power at work when keen Christians tried to mould other people under pressure so that they conformed to a standard pattern of 'holiness'? Was it really his prompting that impelled people to travel the world claiming to be universal teachers, with a 'prophetic ministry' to tell everyone else what to do?

Last night I'd made a list of all the times I could think of when I'd resisted God's word to me because of the difficulty I had in trusting the Holy Spirit to guide me. Fear had always been a major obstacle. I knew it wasn't an ordinary psychological anxiety state because I could get on with ordinary life quite easily; the fear only ever affected my response to God. I was afraid of the Holy Spirit because I was afraid of being deceived by counterfeits. That fear

74

was locking me up into frozen immobility as effectively as icebergs surrounding an arctic ship. 'What is frozen, gently warm', we sang at Pentecost. But I couldn't let the Spirit of Pentecost get near me; I was too well protected by my own self-defence system against all spiritual influence. Only God's love could get rid of my fear, and my fear came between me and him like a great wall of ice. 'Generosity to God is the key,' I thought. 'That's why I couldn't identify myself with the woman.' I could, as a Protestant, imagine myself united with the crucified Christ, dying with him as an individual. But I couldn't see myself as part of his body when it appeared in the sinful, human form of the Church on earth.

Could I do that now? I had learned by experience not to trust those who claimed to be inspired by the Holy Spirit but who condemned the institutions of the Church. Could I trust a representative of a Church that my whole upbringing had conditioned me to believe was closed to the Holy Spirit's leading? Could I trust the director to give me the help I needed to find the true, genuine, Holy Spirit of God? I decided that I would simply tell him what had happened and let him say what he thought I should do about it. When he arrived I gave him a brief account of yesterday's prayer. I told him that I knew God was calling me closer to himself in prayer and service, but my own fear always seemed to get in the way. I couldn't respond to God's love as I wanted to, because of the barrier there seemed to be between us. I *knew* that Jesus had broken down the barrier, I said, and I really was 'converted' in my intentions at least; but I couldn't get past the wall of ice and it wouldn't go away, not even when I thought about Jesus dying for me on the cross. When I'd finished telling him he asked if I'd mind him praying for me. I knelt down, and he prayed quite simply that God would deliver me from fear and set me free to serve him. It was all very gentle and undramatic. But that dreadful, numbing fear went, as if the wall of ice was melting and the blocks were dropping off, all through that day.

I knew then that the gospel really is good news. God does have the power to save people from whatever oppresses them and keeps them in chains, opposed to his will for them. I'd known about God's love before and I'd tasted it for myself. But I needed to be set free before I could more fully respond to it. I had been told many times before that Jesus did set people free, and I'd believed it and trusted that he could indeed free me. But God's power had actually reached me through the prayer of another Christian, and a Christian right outside my own tradition. The body of Christ was indeed broken and battered by our sinful divisions, but it was still the body of Christ, in which the power of the Holy Spirit was at work. It was a truth which I was to realize more deeply through the day's prayer.

The theme for the third day was the mystery of the incarnation: God the Son taking human flesh and being born as man (*Spiritual Exercises* nos 101-9). God the Trinity is beyond all images. But Jesus is the image of the invisible God and all our images find their truth in him, including the images of my own imagination. Because of this, St Ignatius presents the truth of the incarnation in *visual* form, as something to be looked at first and only thought about afterwards. The text of the *Spiritual Exercises* looks very complicated at this point, but none of the *Exercises* make any sense if you simply read them. In order to know what they mean you have to do them. And in order to do them you need a reliable guide. My director interpreted the text by suggesting that I should look at the truth of God's coming into the world in the same way that medieval painters looked at the truths of Scripture, painting different parts of the same story all together on the panels of their altarpieces.

I found this quite easy to do, because I once shared rooms at university with a girl who was studying medieval history. She had passed on to me her enthusiasm for medieval triptychs and illuminated manuscripts; we'd explored the city art gallery together and discovered ancient treasures. But I hadn't expected my own imagination, twenty years later, to act like a medieval painter itself and present the truth in a completely new light, which is what happened. The director had given me three truths to hold together. The first was the mystery and reality of God, which I had encountered on the first day: God who is before and beyond time, to whom all time is present, the source and truth of everything that exists. The Trinity, the director said, is our true person. The second truth was the mystery of sin which I had experienced the previous day: mankind being lost without grace. The third was the particular event in time at which these two universal visions meet: Mary and the angel of the annunciation.

I couldn't imagine God, of course, but I could use the same symbolic representation that the medieval painters used to show the Father, Son and Holy Spirit, and I put that on one side of the picture. I then tried to imagine being lost without grace, by thinking of the worst human circumstances I knew personally. I'd recently been a patient in the accident ward of a large hospital, where there had been people with horrifying injuries. But I couldn't see it without the grace of God. The hospital beds appeared in my imagination against the flat golden background which medieval artists used to show that heaven was behind what was happening on earth. There had been a great deal of love and care and compassion on that ward. I remembered the dedication and skill of the nursing staff, the concern of the patients for each other and the help the more able-bodied gave the others. Even hopeless cases were surrounded by love: a young husband sitting day after day beside his wife; the patients sharing a room with an elderly lady who never spoke but woke screaming every night; the parents of a teenager killed in a road accident. God's grace had been at work there, I thought, amidst the depths of human tragedy, and among people who may not have consciously thought of him at all. God's grace was seen in human lives; there was no place in the world beyond its reach.

As I looked at the picture, the arrangement shifted. God was above it and outside it, like the motif in the centre top of an ornate picture frame, and his grace was streaming down into the picture, making a golden background to the whole world. At the top of the picture, underneath the stylized Trinity in the frame, were Mary and the angel of the annunciation (although I hadn't consciously imagined them), almost as if that were a lens to refract the golden light of grace. All the world in the main frame of the picture was going about its business against the background of that light, just as I'd seen it in the valley the evening before. 'God is above time,' I thought, 'redeeming the time.' I opened the New Testament at St

Luke's account of the annunciation. That, too, took the form of a composite picture as I read it, like Early Renaissance paintings I'd seen. Mary and the angel were looking at each other, like the figures in the Fra Angelico fresco in Florence, but instead of the arcade behind them there was the flat gold background again, like a Sienese School miniature of the annunciation I remembered from my student days.

I closed the New Testament and looked at the picture in my imagination. As I looked, Mary and the angel came forward out of the gold background like cardboard cut-out figures, still looking at each other, and came inside me. It was all very gentle and peaceful, even if rather odd. I asked the Lord what it meant. There was a great sense of his love all around me.

'In order to have her response,' he said, 'you have to have her within you.' I needed to think about that, being a Protestant, and I stayed with those words for some time, until I began to have some understanding of what they might mean. St Paul wrote to the Galatians that the fruit of the Spirit is love, joy, peace, gentleness, patience, kindness, faithfulness, meekness and temperance (Gal. 5. 22-3). These fruits were evident in the world, but they came from God's Spirit. That same Holy Spirit was at work in me. But in order for the fruit of the Spirit to grow properly in my life I needed to respond, as Mary did, 'Behold the handmaid of the Lord; be it done to me according to your word' (Luke 1. 38). Being the servant of the Lord wasn't just something you *did*; it needn't be anything you did at all. Being the servant of the Lord meant accepting God's word into your life and responding to it, allowing it to change you and bringing forth the character of Jesus. I couldn't respond like that without God's grace. And God's grace to respond came to me through other people.

'We need each other,' I thought. I'd needed the director's prayer today. The light of God's grace shone through places like this house; I'd needed the whole community here in order to make a retreat in the first place. I was dependent on other people's response to God. Perhaps that was what Catholics meant when they said that we were dependent on Mary for our salvation. It didn't mean that she took the place of her Son. It meant she could have said 'no'. It was God's grace which enabled her to say 'yes', and that 'yes' enabled God's grace to come into the world for everyone. And that grace redeems the past. We're bound up with our own ideas of time, I thought, but God is above time and *he* redeems time past. My own time past can be redeemed when I say 'yes' to him now. And I can say 'yes' because of God's grace coming to me through other people's obedience.

I could never be alone in my response to God. Other people carried me in their prayer. Other people were entitled to concern themselves with my response to God because I am part of the whole body of Christ, and whatever I do affects the health and strength of the whole - like every other part. I would never even have seen the truth of the incarnation like this if I had not been here. The Catholic way of seeing truth corrected my own partial understanding. But it wasn't 'Catholic' versus 'Protestant' any more: it was faith and response, or unbelief. Jesus was with me and in me. It was he who was promising to work in me by his Spirit to bring forth the fruit he wanted. I was very conscious of being in touch with other Christians and upheld by their prayers, of being one branch of the whole vine. I was also conscious of the Lord's presence with me, and with us all.

The final suggestion for prayer was: 'I will think what I ought to say to the Three Divine Persons, or to the eternal Word Incarnate, or to His Mother, our Lady. According to the light that I have received, I will beg for grace to follow and imitate more closely our Lord (*Spiritual Exercises* no. 109). I decided that 'according to the light I had received' I should have to swallow my Protestant prejudices and address Mary. Could I ask her for help just as I'd asked the director for help earlier on? No Protestant is comfortable about praying to anyone other than God, but I found it very hard to ask help from other Christians who got things wrong almost as often as I did. Perhaps that was why it was good to ask help from those who are transparent to God because they obey him themselves. Mary had become part of my own imaginative reality. I decided to ask her for all the fruits of the Spirit that she had and I didn't: gentleness, meekness, patience and humility. If I had those, I might stand more chance of responding to God.

'I have nothing that my Son did not give me,' she said. 'Here he comes; he will give them himself.'

I don't know how to describe what happened next because it was as if it was outside my imagination, with everything going on around me like one of those fairy stories where the hero goes through an ordinary door and finds himself in an alternative, parallel world. We were in a meadow of grass and little flowers, the kind of meadow you find high up in the Alps with the same almost irridescent green grass and brilliant white light. Only this was much brighter than that. And brighter still was the Lord, coming over the grass towards us, all light and love. He was too bright to look at directly. I hung on to Mary's hand. I was terrified.

'It's all right,' she said.

He came up to me, and put a cloak of a shimmering sort of silver stuff on my shoulders and a glittering circlet on my head. And then the whole thing faded as quickly as it had happened.

'What on earth did it mean?' I wondered as the ordinary room came back into focus. One thing I was quite sure about: it did *not* mean that I was a spiritual super-hero. There were advantages to being a Protestant, I thought; we knew that *all* Christians were called to be saints and *all* Christians were 'saints' already in God's sight. Of course that was what it meant. I remembered what the psalmists had said about what God does for his people: 'He crowns you with love and mercy' (Ps. 103.4), and I began to understand. The psalmists had experienced it too, and they'd put it into poetry for all God's people. Whatever anybody knows from true experience is true for everyone by faith, because we are all one body and share each other's gifts. The psalmists spoke about God being clothed in majesty and glory, and wrapped in a robe of light (Ps. 104. 1-2). They prayed that the priests of Israel would be clothed with righteousness and salvation (Ps. 132.9). And all believers were priests in this sense. I felt sure that I was on the right track. God had answered the director's prayer and set me free from the fear that kept me from him. Now I was restored to the relationship which all Christians have with their Lord. It is Christ's character which is our new character, and we are given it like an armour of light to put on over all our human failings and faults, as a gift

80

(Rom. 13. 12-14; Eph. 6. 11-17; Col. 3. 10-14). I could let the Holy Spirit mould my life to that character, by responding to his prompting day by day and by turning away from everything that denied it. And all Christians are crowned with the Lord's faithful love - his grace - which keeps them in a relationship with him even when they do not sense his presence or understand what is happening, and even when in their ignorance they are resisting him. What I had just seen was a vivid picture of the relationship between *all* Christians and their Lord. And this relationship is his gift. That, too, the psalmist knew:

> Bless the Lord, O my soul, and all that is within me,
> bless his holy name!
> Bless the Lord, O my soul, and forget not all his benefits,
> Who forgives all your iniquity,
> Who heals all your diseases,
> Who redeems your life from the Pit,
> Who crowns you with steadfast love and mercy,
> Who satisfies you with good as long as you live
> so that your youth is restored like the eagle's. (Ps. 103. 1-5)

That was what renewal meant, I thought. I began to see how even a broken, divided community could be a channel of God's love to me, because all the people in it could by faith be in that relationship with him, however imperfect they were. Christ's character could cover all our faults if we only let him give it to us. Jesus grew up within a human community that had just as many divisions within it as the Christian Church has today. That community formed his thinking in ways we can never fully understand but can glimpse from what scholars have discovered about the various traditions within Judaism at that time. In all that formation, Jesus never once failed to respond to his Father. And during his public ministry he began to form a community to be the new Israel. His apostles would know the truth of salvation and proclaim it to the world, not only by what they said but by what they were and what they did as the Holy Spirit's fire transformed them into the true image of God's love which they proclaimed. The world still needs to see a true, visible alternative to the human societies of the world which are bound into enmity with God and divided against themselves. Christians are called to make the true city of God visible on earth.

The Old Testament talks about God's people as the 'virgin Israel' and the 'daughter of Jerusalem'. Mary was the living embodiment of that vision of God's people, wholly responsive to him as God's people as a whole never were in all their long history. Her response was made possible by the same God who took flesh from her. But that union of God with human nature was not brought about without great pain. 'A sword shall pierce your own heart,' Simeon had told her as she presented the infant Jesus in the Temple. Perhaps the same was true, in a reflected way, for all Christians' experience of union with God and with each other.

My own understanding of salvation had been far too narrow. Salvation is never a solitary affair between me and God. It begins with the secret response of a human heart opening to God's love in silence. But it does not end until the whole people of God is transformed into the likeness of his Son, bound together in love like the love within the threefold life of God, revealing his glory to the whole world. At the end of the Book of Revelation, when all evil is finally conquered and all murderers and liars have been overcome by the victory of the Lamb, the true vision of salvation appears. The holy city comes down from the new heaven to the new earth, clothed with the good deeds of the saints: God's true bride. In that city heaven and earth are joined in union and fruitfulness is brought to all Creation:

> I saw no temple in the city, for its temple is the Lord God Almighty and the Lamb. . . . Then he showed me the river of the water of life, bright as crystal, flowing from the throne of God and of the Lamb through the middle of the street of the city; also on either side of the river, the tree of life with its twelve kinds of fruit, yielding its fruit each month; and the leaves of the tree were for the healing of the nations. There shall no more be anything accursed, but the throne of God and the Lamb shall be in it, and his servants shall worship him; they shall see his face, and his name shall be on their foreheads. (Rev. 21.22; 22.1–4)

That is what salvation means. I might think that I was taking risks in responding to God. But God has taken the greatest risk of all in committing himself to human life and waiting for human response. The Son of God entered human life in order to bring human beings back to the joy of eternal life pictured in the Book of Revelation. And that gift was given in the moment when a young Jewish village girl said 'yes' to the voice of her calling.

Note

1. St Ignatius' 'Rules For Thinking With the Church' no. 13 (*Spiritual Exercises* no. 365) sets out the principle that the Holy Spirit guides individuals *and* the Church, but the Church has the power of veto on individual inspirations.

8 · The Voice of this Calling

Follow me, and I will make you become fishers of men (MARK 1.17)

The good news is that God has entered human history in order to set people free, to restore them to his friendship and to bring them to eternal happiness in the new creation with Jesus at its head. This alone is the true gospel of salvation, and the whole Church is commissioned to proclaim it in word and action. But not only are there false gospels on offer. There are false ways of making the true gospel known, so that the message of God's love is obscured. Ten years previously, when we'd been living in Liverpool, I'd walked through the city centre just before Christmas and been struck by the huge variety of alternative gospels on offer, and also by the way the true gospel was distorted when it became one more facet of our culture's celebration of commerce. Jesus was tempted to compel belief by appearing as a superman figure, he was tempted to give surface contentment by short-cut satisfaction of material needs without reference to God's will for the world, and he was tempted to make unholy alliances with the powers at work against God. We didn't seem to have learned from his experience of overcoming temptation, I thought. I'd written a poem about our own denials in practice of the truth we proclaimed, that the Word of God was made flesh for our salvation.

> Turkeys and beer are not enough
> to feed the spirit. Stronger stuff
> displays for sale: the arcane book,
> forbidden knowledge, herbs and stars,
> the secrets of the universe,
> the apple that we took.

And saffron robes sweep down the street;
rival messiahs smiling meet:
Children of God and Sons of Light
follow their independent ways.
Their incandescent ecstasies
flow out into the night.

O give the word: conjure from air
the bread of life. The need is there.
Untouched by human hand, O see
manna from heaven wrapped and sold
as cheaply as the Word of old:
thirty new pence, or free.

The poem had been a protest about what Dietrich Bonhoeffer
called 'cheap grace' being offered as if the Lord's death for our
salvation were some celestial sleight-of-hand which brought us
salvation without our having to respond in any way. Christian faith
was reduced to believing a set of verbal formulae set out in free
tracts and cheap booklets that people could buy over a counter
without ever coming into contact with Christians who lived their
faith out in the world. Our efforts at evangelizing the unchurched
seemed to be on the level of the plastic mangers and star of
Bethlehem illuminations in the shop windows and streets. I'd
brought that poem with me because I didn't think I'd got any
further than that in the ten years since I'd written it. Now I
wondered whether the truth of the incarnation which I had
experienced in a new way yesterday was the focus of that search for
a true proclamation of the gospel as well as the search for the truth
of renewal in the Church.

As I was thinking over how best to describe my previous day's
prayer to the director, the picture of the medieval altarpiece came
back to mind as vividly as I had imagined it yesterday. The golden
background was still there, but it seemed as though someone had
stamped out circles in it, as a child might stamp out circles of
pastry, leaving widely spaced holes. On the bare wood of each circle
was painted a human figure. The golden light of God's grace shone

all around these figures, I thought, but it did not touch them. That was how I'd been before the director prayed for me: knowing God's grace was there but unable to receive it because I was locked up in fear. As I looked I was drawn into the picture in my imagination and stood in the centre of it, surrounded by the people in their empty circles. The words came into my head, 'apostle to your people', a phrase I didn't remember hearing before, and then I was on the other side of the panel, where the symbol of the Trinity was painted, and the Trinity was saying, 'Who shall we send, and who will go for us?' just the same as in the Old Testament story of Isaiah's vision in the Temple (Isaiah 6). I'd read that story so often that I didn't have to think about my response: it came out almost automatically. 'Here am I; send me.'

I thought about that and wondered what it meant. Isaiah was a prophet. He received a prophet's call: to make God's true word known to his own people who would not receive it. But Christians know the Word incarnate. Apostles are called to receive the word of God in Jesus, to be made flesh again in a new situation. Jesus Christ is alive and works through the members of his body. But what did it mean to be an apostle to your *own* people? As if in reply to my wondering, the first verses of St John's Gospel came back to mind again: 'He came to his own people, and his own people did not receive him.' Would it be the same for me?

There was no more time for any further reflection because the director was knocking on the door for our morning interview. I told him that his prayer for me on Sunday had been answered and he seemed relieved. Then I told him about seeing the annunciation picture and what had happened. I also told him about the need to relate the gospel to ordinary daily life and the poem I'd written, but I didn't tell him about what had happened just now; I wanted more time to think about it. But then, rather to my surprise, I found myself pouring out all the problems I'd had with relating *prayer* to everyday life, which centred round the book I'd remembered on Sunday: *The Cloud of Unknowing*.

I'd first read the book about twelve years previously, when I really did want to grow closer to God and before fear started to get in the way. I could understand the way the author spoke about prayer, directing one's whole heart and mind to God in love, without many words. That book appealed to a desire hidden deep inside me, which I recognized as the same sort of desire that had led me into the Anglican Church. But it was packed with warnings of the dangers threatening people who began this way of prayer without being called to it. Presumption like this could end up in a state of total delusion, so that people were unable to love God at all, even when they thought that this was what they were doing. There was a true simplicity of a childlike heart living in love and trusting dependence on God. But there was also a false simplicity which denied all human reactions and produced zombies who were numb to the pain of the world. People like this thought they were loving God in this state when all the time it had been themselves they were loving.

All in all it seemed that I would have been well advised to forget about *The Cloud of Unknowing* and go back to Christopher Robin. 'God bless Mummy, I know that's right' might not be exactly satisfying as adult prayer, but it was certainly safe enough. Yet I couldn't forget *The Cloud*. That book had captured my imagination as no book on prayer had ever done before or since. I took my presumption in both hands and hoped the Lord would overlook the fact that I was none of the things that the author said one should be before beginning this prayer. I was neither humble nor disciplined; I was not even penitent on his terms. He'd written before the Reformation divided the Western Church, but even in his day there had been people who recommended Bible study for all and sit light to the Church's penitential system. Evangelicals saw them as their founding fathers. The author of *The Cloud* quite clearly considered them to be heretics. In order to be penitent on *his* terms I'd have to renounce my Protestant past and accept the penitential discipline of the Roman Catholic Church. And there was no way I could do that: it would deny everything that God had done in my life from childhood upwards.

The problem with traditions that refuse to accept you as you are is that you are forced to pick out the bits you *can* assimilate and leave the bits you cannot. But the problem with doing this is that you do not have all the background knowledge you need in order to understand what you are doing; and more important, you do not have other people to help you. And I had needed help. Sometimes God was real as never before. At other times my imagination threw up strings of irrelevant images, unrolling like a surrealist ballet across my mental screen and dissipating all my intention to direct mind and heart to God. Sometimes the images were horrible and even frightening. Mostly, though, when I did set aside a time for prayer and stick to it, I had a blank depressing struggle with the boredom of sitting there by myself with no sign of God at all. If I tried to pray sitting in a comfortable chair I often went to sleep. If I knelt on the floor I got cramp in my legs after about ten minutes. And there were weeks on end when I gave up the struggle altogether and settled for saying the set order for Morning Prayer with Rob, because I could say the words without having to think about them.

I couldn't see where the love of God came into all this at all. Neither could I see how to relate this way of prayer to the Lord's commission to proclaim the good news of salvation which all Evangelicals take as their charter text. It was a beguiling thought that God could work through you in ways you never knew in the course of this kind of prayer, but I wasn't at all sure it was true. Perhaps it was true for saints in the Catholic sense, but not for saints in the Protestant sense who were still far from fully sanctified. And even thinking of this kind of prayer as intercession was fraught with difficulty. If sitting still for half an hour let you off the obligation to give practical help to those in need and to speak the word of God, then you might as well forget about Christianity and take up a less demanding religion in which you could beam happy thoughts to the world at large without getting your hands dirty.

I had problems with contemplative prayer because it was rooted in a Catholic tradition from whose point of view I appeared as a heretic. 'Praying in the Spirit' was part of the Pentecostal tradition: praying in tongues, to be precise. And I couldn't see how *that* related to the commission to proclaim the good news either. I knew that it was God who had given me that gift of prayer and I honestly did not want to devalue it. But it was very difficult not to when there were people who extolled it as the answer to Life, the Universe, and Everything. Some people quoted St Paul to the effect that it was a gift for building up Christians spiritually, and concluded that those who had not been given it were thereby doomed to arrested spiritual development. There were apocryphal stories about preachers in foreign parts arriving at their destination and using their gift of prayer in the pulpit when the translator failed to show up; it was claimed that the audience understood the word of God that was spoken. I'd had to learn Swahili the hard way, and I wasn't all that fluent in it even after eight years. Whatever happened at Pentecost, I thought, the book of Acts was quite clear that the assembly understood the disciples to be praising God in many different, known languages: the reverse of Babel's curse. It was also clear that Peter used the occasion to proclaim the gospel of Jesus in a language that everyone understood, and not in unintelligible gobbledegook. As for those who claimed to be superior to the Jesus portrayed in the Gospels because praying in tongues was one of the 'greater works' than the works he did, if it was not Jesus who was doing the works in them one might question whether it was his Spirit inspiring them. Praying in tongues seemed just as open to error as praying in silence.

That left praying in ordinary English, which I had to admit I felt safest with. I had to be careful that I wasn't simply giving God a shopping list, but I could get over that by using canticles and psalms of praise and adoration, and making my petitions in the words of the Lord's Prayer. Jesus did not give his disciples any instruction on the 'technique' of prayer as the Greek teachers of religious philosophy did, and he did not promise them ecstatic experience either. He took the ordinary Jewish forms of prayer with which his disciples had been familiar from childhood, and transformed them into a model of Christian prayer which is all about living as children of God in the world. The Lord's Prayer, like the *Spiritual Exercises*, begins with a statement of intent to put the person praying into the context of his true relationship with God. He is my Father - *our* Father - loving me and all his children and ready to hear and answer us all. He is in heaven, and other than us, so that my attitude to him is worship and wonder. And all my petitions are directed by the prayer 'Thy Kingdom come'. 'Man was created to praise, reverence and serve God our Lord,' said St Ignatius (no. 23). The Lord's Prayer begins by setting my own life in that context.

I had found that praying the Lord's Prayer did help me to get my life into the true perspective. When I prayed for God's Kingdom to come, I stated my belief that the kingdom of the world is transient and God's values are those which will last. That is why I could pray for my daily bread, handing over all my concerns to a God who is in control of the physical as well as the spiritual processes of the world. My experience had to catch up with my intention here, as in the prayer 'forgive us ... as we forgive', but at least praying this regularly did remind me that God is judge, not me. The Lord's Prayer was the antidote to many of the false spirits that sent 'renewal' spinning down the wrong path. If I prayed 'lead us not into temptation' I would be less likely to give way to the urge to indulge in spiritual heroics. The only way that I could fight at all was under the cross of Christ, with his victory for my own protection. I knew I had to fight in his way if I was to conquer evil in my own life.

But it was one thing to be able to see straight while I was praying the Lord's Prayer. It was quite another to maintain that vision of God's Kingdom once I got behind a desk or went shopping or sat on a committee. I could be dragged back into judging for myself what was good and evil and wanting to oppose the evil by force; I could be beguiled by the world in disguise as it tempted me to promote God's Kingdom using the world's methods. Somehow I needed to be able to see straight in my daily life.

I don't remember now how much of all this I was able to explain, but the director heard me out without comment. And then the last thing that I'd expected: he recalled me to that original direction to the kind of prayer described in *The Cloud of Unknowing*. I spluttered something about needing to be earthed, but he simply said, 'God is calling you to this. Off you go.' So I then had to think out how I was going to do it in my life as it was, rather than tell myself that I couldn't do it because I was an Evangelical and not a

Roman Catholic nun. I would have to ask God for light on how this way of praying connected with the Lord's Prayer, and how his call to me to pray like this related with his call to be an 'apostle to your people' - whatever that meant. It seemed a lot to expect from one day's prayer. But as soon as I looked at my prayer in the light of the Word made flesh I began to see how phoney prayer, whether it was contemplative or charismatic or evangelical, denied that central fact of faith.

I didn't understand it all on that day, of course. But as I reflected in the months after the retreat I did begin to see the difference between true and false prayer. Phoney contemplation denied the reality of my life in the world and denied the need to express love in practical action. Phoney charismatic prayer had the same effect. It denied the interdependence of all Christians in the body of Christ and claimed that some possessed the Spirit in a way others didn't - like spiritual 'healers' who were exalted at the expense of those who spent their working lives washing bedpans and changing dressings. Phoney evangelical prayer told God at length exactly what was wrong with his world and how he ought to go about putting things right; it could even call down judgement on those who opposed 'God's work' - the work which was indistinguishable from my own human efforts. But Jesus preached *and* healed. He reached out to all the lost sheep of Israel who were ignored by the spiritual élite of his day. He did not pass final judgement but died so that the world which had opposed his mission might find salvation. The opposition of the world was the very means by which God's Kingdom was thrown open to all mankind.

It took me a long time to understand this. But that day, in retreat, I did begin to see my own life in the light of the life of God's Son on earth. I was failing to live the gospel I professed to believe because I had not trusted God to be with me in my own circumstances in England. In some ways it had been much easier in Tanzania to live by faith. External circumstances were much more difficult there: there were food shortages and epidemics and the constant battle to overcome the lack of facilities which in England we took for granted. But we had felt that we were all in the same circumstances together. The missionary society, we knew, would not let us starve, even though one dismal week we had nothing to eat except boiled cassava – and the cassava had seen happier days, too. The point was that in Tanzania we were not immune from the troubles which afflicted the local people and made living by faith difficult for everyone. We were all sharing the same struggle to find God's will in our daily lives, and there was no false split in local Christians' minds between worship in church on Sunday and love and concern for their neighbours from Monday to Saturday.

In England we had found it much more difficult, because we *weren't* in the same boat. We had spent a great deal of energy in Tanzania building up trust between the Housing Department and the local self-builders so that they knew we didn't see them as 'problems' to be solved but as fellow-workers in building the city. But back in England, we ourselves fell into the category of people defined as 'social problems'. We were a statistic of 'rural poverty'; we lived in a sub-standard cottage with nine-inch brick walls, one cold water tap and a chemical loo. We had enjoyed camping there for years before we went overseas; but now that it was our permanent home, I began to view it with the eyes of my society. The brambles in the garden were ten feet high. The place needed scrubbing from top to bottom and painting, and my neck was still not right so that I found it hard even to scour a saucepan, let alone paint a ceiling. We had no cupboards to put our clutter away in. Five of us were living in two and a half habitable rooms. By all the standards of our own British society, we were thoroughly deprived, and there was no way out of our circumstances without far more money than we seemed ever likely to earn. The end of our final leave with the missionary society was in sight, and we still had no work and no prospect of any. I wouldn't have minded if I hadn't felt that we were a 'problem' to our fellow Christians as well as to the nation. Everyone seemed to be talking about 'the poor' and 'the unemployed', and how 'we' can help 'them' – mainly, it seemed, by lobbying parliament. They *talked* about 'partners in mission', I thought crossly. But we didn't feel like partners at all, more like grubby poor relations who couldn't be allowed into the drawing room. And we were grubby. Seen from the perspective of normal British society, our way of life was unbelievably squalid.

The subject of the day's prayer was the nativity (*Spiritual Exercises* nos 110-117), and the director had again suggested that I didn't think about it so much as look at it, letting the truth of it penetrate my whole mind and heart. The preliminary prayer was similar to the prayer in *The Cloud of Unknowing*: it was directing heart and mind to God. 'Beg God Our grace', St Ignatius had written, 'that all my intentions, actions and operations may be directed purely to the praise and service of His Divine Majesty.' The prayer for *grace* struck me. Until then I hadn't paid much attention to this almost conventional beginning to each period of prayer I made. But today I realized that although I regularly prayed 'cleanse the thoughts of our hearts by the inspiration of your Holy Spirit', I had been trying to direct my own intention to God by myself. No wonder I hadn't succeeded, when I needed God's grace even to begin. Of course he'd given me his grace; but I'd never before seriously considered what asking for it meant. By beginning any prayer with this prayer for grace, I can accept whatever happens in it as within God's purpose for me. That makes all the difference between true and phoney contemplation. Without God's grace I can never be sure that clouds of unknowing aren't simply smog. But with God's grace I could understand what St Ignatius meant by 'contemplation' of the gospel. The day's prayer with the image of the nativity before my eyes linked my intention to direct mind and heart to God with the reality of my daily life in a very concrete way.

I looked at the scene of the birth of Jesus in my imagination. There was no particularly vivid imagery, but only an ordinary cowshed of the wattle-and-mud variety I'd seen in Tanzania, ankle-deep in cow-dung, with the acrid smell that I knew well. *His* early circumstances were pretty squalid too, I thought. I had been feeling like a stranger in my own country. He was born into a poor working family in an occupied country, part of a vast foreign empire. Mary and Joseph did not even have control over the circumstances of his birth. Perhaps my children would survive without all the things that we were told were necessary for their education and spiritual development but which we could not afford. And perhaps Joseph found it hard to get work too, so far from where anyone knew him or would trust his professional competence to do a proper job. Trusting God didn't mean that you had no worries at all, either in Tanzania or Bethelehem. Perhaps trusting God was compatible with the diminishments of poverty in England. It meant that you trusted God *in* trouble, not that you trusted him to keep you out of it. The picture of the nativity put my ideas of my own life into a different perspective. I would have objected to the conditions under which Joseph and Mary had to carry out *their* mission. The Lord of heaven and earth was born in a smelly cattle pen.

Our Christmas carols say this. I had always thought that our Christmas cards glamorized it. But at the same time as I saw my own life as if it were superimposed on the Gospel scene, I saw also that those traditional paintings which clothe the Virgin in velvet held a deeper insight. Through the pain and degradation of his birth in those conditions floated the words of a carol called 'I sing of a maiden':

> He came all so still
> Where His Mother was,
> As dew in April
> That falleth on the grass

And faintly at first, then more clearly, like a colour slide projected onto patterned wallpaper and gradually focused, the golden angels of the nativity covered the dung-filled straw. The image of a Renaissance painting was superimposed on the stable scene. All pain and all poverty are now transfigured by his presence in them.

Could I believe this? My head sometimes felt as if it would drop off any minute. Unless work came in soon we should have nothing to live on when our leave ended. Could I trust God even if the pain went on and we had no work? Suddenly I knew I could. It was not perhaps a very solid trust, but it was a start. 'OK,' I said to the Lord. 'I *think* you have led us to where we are now. We may be mistaken, and if so I can trust you to show us that too. So now I want to hand you my fear of pain and poverty, because I can't get rid of it by myself and it's getting in the way of my seeing straight.'

I went down to supper feeling more lighthearted than I had done for months. During the meal my husband rang up with some necessary business, apologizing for disturbing my retreat. It was the first time he'd been able to ring from home, he told me then, because the telephone had only been connected that afternoon. And a funny thing happened. As soon as the engineer replaced the receiver after his test call, the phone rang again. The caller was the senior partner of the practice we'd left to go to Tanzania. He'd been working on his own since Rob left the parnership and he now had a sudden glut of work. Would Rob help him out?

It could of course have been coincidence. But I felt suddenly exhilarated. We'd come to expect that kind of coincidence in answer to our prayers during our time in Tanzania, when we'd had to trust God for all our daily needs because we had very little control over our circumstances. Was God telling me that I really *could* live by faith here in Britain as well? Was he showing me that the way my society saw poverty was not necessarily the way he saw it? If so, then I could accept my present circumstances as his gift, given for his own good purpose which I might not know now. I could trust him for what I really needed, not only in my external life but also in my inner life. Bringing myself to him in silence each day was simply a way of expressing that trust. And if I could live by faith and trust in the middle of my poverty – which was not really poverty at all by Tanzanian standards – then *that* would witness to the truth of the gospel better than anything I could say.

I knew that I should have to pray for the grace, daily, to live like this in faith and trust. As I reviewed the day's prayer after supper the words of the psalm I'd read in the morning came back to mind: 'The Lord looks down from heaven, he sees the whole human race' (Ps. 33.13 JB). It was the same Lord who had called me to be an apostle to my own people, bringing the gospel to those who shared the circumstances of my own life. That was what he called all Christians to do, sooner or later. I needn't think I was alone in an alien land. The Lord had many other people who had not been sucked up into our society's values and its 'success ethic'. We were all part of his one mission to save the world, and he was inviting me, as he invited all his people, to share the conditions which he accepted himself. I should never have known that my relative poverty in England could be good if I had not experienced his presence shining out in it. But once I had experienced this I knew that I couldn't tell people who are out of work in Britain that God loves them and has a purpose for them, when society sees them as a problem and values them as useless - unless I could show them that God's love for me did not depend on whether I was successful in human terms. I couldn't tell people who worried about whether their housekeeping money would stretch the whole week that God could be trusted to provide - unless I knew that my own security did not rest in insurance and pension schemes. Perhaps that was my only job at the moment: to learn to trust God in the conditions which my society feared almost more than it feared to die.

> The eye of the Lord is on those who fear him
> on those who rely on his love,
> to rescue their souls from death,
> and keep them alive in famine...
> (Ps. 33.18f JB)

'Lord,' I prayed in the words of the psalm's last verse, 'let your love rest on us, as our hope rests on you.' My basic need was not more things. It was the grace for which I'd been praying all day: a deeper knowledge of the Lord himself made man for me. I'd received that grace today and I thanked God for it, because I could now see that it was the centre of all Christian contemplative life and the foundation for all service and witness in the world. Putting God's call to prayer first in my life would keep that need of grace always in mind. God might also call me to undertake a special task for him as well, and I had to be ready to obey that call too, if it came. But I did not have to worry if it did not.

9 · Soldiers of Christ

And they have conquered him by the blood of the Lamb and by the word of their testimony, for they loved not their lives even unto death (REV. 12.11)

Two world wars and the threat of nuclear annihilation have made Christians understandably nervous about using traditional military imagery to express the nature of spiritual combat. But spiritual combat goes on in all Christians' lives. As soon as anyone turns from simply drifting with the tide of the society around him and seriously begins to live the gospel in a world which rejects the incarnate Word, he finds himself pitched into a conflict between the life the Lord is calling him to live and the world's values. Christ does bring peace to our lives when we turn to him. But this peace does not mean that there is no more struggle: quite the reverse. The war between Christ and Satan is real and serious, and it is quite irresponsible to underestimate it.

In the past Christians sometimes mistook the battlefront and fought each other instead of fighting evil. They still make the same mistake, even if they do not use swords and cannonballs these days and are much more gentlemanly about it. But St Ignatius helps everyone who prays the *Spiritual Exercises* to see exactly where the fight is centred. He helped me, a Protestant, to understand the nature of the physical wars and violence in the past between Protestants and Catholics. The same temptations that beset Christians in the past beset me, too. If there was one single thing that I learned from that retreat, it was how to recognize the real enemy I was fighting. Jesus told parables about discernment. There were weeds in the wheat which could be allowed to grow up with the crop until harvest sorted them out. There were also wolves which carried off the lambs and tore the sheep to bits, and they certainly could *not* be allowed to grow up with the flock, but ought to be shot on sight. I learned a lot about how to tell wolves from sheepdogs.

Discernment of the enemy is absolutely crucial to Christian warfare and is central to the *Spiritual Exercises*. The combat presupposes a knowledge of my own sin from which I have been rescued by Christ, and some knowledge of the Lord and a willingness in principle to answer his call to follow him and serve him in the world. I also need to know my own dependence on God's grace both in order to see clearly and for the strength to put vision into practical effect. Jesus calls all his disciples sooner or later to take the good news of God's Kingdom into enemy territory. In order to do this they have to recognize the enemy's tactics. There are no international treaties to demarcate the boundary between 'The Church' and 'The World'. The Lord's call is a call to continuous conflict, more like guerilla operations than trench warfare, where the battle may be fought and won or lost within my own local Christian group, within my own family and within myself. Everyone who responds to the Lord's call commits himself to the conditions of service that all combat troops expect: periods of training; regular discipline; constant vigilance. Like most Anglicans I find it quite bracing to think about this during Lent, when I make an annual attack on bad habits and lethargy. But the battle goes on all the year round. Being confident of the ultimate outcome does not protect me from defeat now. I need to be able to see and recognize Jesus in all the decisions I have to make in daily life. God's gift which enables me to do this is given in the victory that Jesus won once and for all on the cross. I can't do God's work without accepting *that* as my standard. If I try, I may well end up fighting on the wrong side.

There seem to be two main ways in which Christians get things wrong in the Church today in the western world, and they are rather like the ways they got things wrong in the second century of the Church's life, when all the original apostles had died and those who had known them personally were elderly. It was a time when the cultural background to everyone's lives was changing very fast, as it is today. There was a general feeling of insecurity as the peace of the Empire was threatened from outside by hostile neighbours and from inside by economic depression. I wouldn't have connected that period with our own, as I didn't know much about it, but for the coincidence which laid me flat on my back in bed reading books about early Church History at the same time as some of our local charismatics were claiming the direct guidance of the Holy Spirit for activities which even the most sympathetic observer might question. It struck me then that there were charismatics who got things spectacularly wrong in the second century. And I wondered whether there wasn't a modern counterpart also to the other group of Christians who got things wrong then by diluting their faith in Jesus with too much of the contemporary 'counter-culture'.

Could I learn from the ancient past in order to understand the present? The charismatics I'd met who claimed to have got past the 'theology of the cross' so that they were living by the Spirit in the New Age seemed very similar to the second-century Montanists whose founder Montanus claimed to possess the Holy Spirit in exactly the same sense that Jesus was the incarnate Word of God.[1] I'd met neo-gnostics, as well: in the Christian 'fringe' in England before we'd gone overseas, through books I'd read, and even in the African Christian sub-culture where traditional religions and Christian faith came together and challenged and influenced each other. Some of these people seemed to be completely outside any church; some were respected figures right at the Church's centre. In this the neo-gnostic movement seemed very like the original one and, just like the original Gnostics of the first Christian centuries, the modern ones claimed to have been initiated into a spirituality of inner knowledge much higher than the crudely literal beliefs which focused faith on the Jesus of Nazareth pictured in the four New Testament Gospels. That kind of faith might be fit for children and people with limited intelligence, they said, but the only canonical Gospel with any message for educated people with spiritual potential was the Gospel of John, and even that had to be comprehensively re-mythologized if modern readers were to comprehend its true, spiritual sense.

I certainly didn't want to discount all spiritual experience, because not only did I know that genuine experience often does lead people to God, but also I found it difficult to imagine how anyone could grow in faith without some personal experience of him. How then could people tell the true from the false? I tried to set out some guidelines for the present based on what I had read about the past. True experience is true for reason as well as imagination: it has meaning, and the meaning can be compared with the witness of the whole of Scripture and checked against the faith of the whole Church. True experience forms people in the likeness of Jesus Christ: the image of his cross puts the phantoms of the world to flight. True experience is a gift to the whole body of Christ: it can therefore be related to the whole and will not evaporate if it is submitted to other Christians for a second opinion. The ancient Montanists and Gnostics failed on all those counts. Both groups supplemented Scripture with their own private revelations which they held to be of equal value. Both of them looked down on the faith of the whole Church, seeing themselves as a superior class of Christians with a hot line to heaven. Neither was in the least like Jesus because he forgave sins and they refused to forgive anyone. The Montanists could not forgive failure or less than perfect sanctity in the Church; the Gnostics thought that forgiveness was the same as understanding, and they applied themselves to the task of the latter in a somewhat idiosyncratic way. And both groups avoided the cross. The Gnostics saw no need for Christians not to be fully integrated both within themselves and with the whole of pagan society: truly spiritual people, they thought, could recognize the worship of the Emperor and of other gods as a valid aspect of mankind's search for the Unknown God. The Montanists went to the opposite extreme and exalted martyrdom as the ultimate sign of sanctity. Other Christians sometimes accused them of courting it. But whether or not it is courted, martyrdom which proves a person's sanctity to himself is not at all the same as the true victory of the cross by which the world is drawn to Jesus. It never occurred to these people to ask God for the grace they needed in order to love and forgive their tormentors. They lacked the one thing they needed to be true Christian martyrs, and their presumption simply served to turn all right-thinking pagans away in disgust from the Christian faith.

I found that the 'Meditation on Two Standards' in the *Spiritual Exercises* (nos 136-147) brought my previous experience of discernment into sharp focus, and helped me recognize more about what was going on around me in the world and what was happening in my own personal life with God. St Ignatius set out two progressions by which Christians can tell the inspirations of the Holy Spirit from the temptations of false spirits of the world, even when the evil spirits are disguised as angels of light. If the inspiration encouraged me to seek God's gifts for my own possession, however spiritual these gifts might be, it was false. I would then be tempted to hang on to these gifts even when God wanted me to do without them for his sake. Then I would be tempted to bask in the flattery which comes from having them, and surround myself with an admiring circle of disciples. The final, fatal step would be pride in my possession and pride in myself for possessing it. Even good inspirations could be corrupted in this way so that a person turns from seeking the sole glory of God to wanting a bit of the glory for himself. He may never realize what is happening until it is too late.

When a person is proud he is impervious to God's grace. God's grace cannot reach him directly, because a proud heart is unable to receive it. And God's grace cannot reach him through other people, because by the time he is proud he will be surrounded by people who agree with everything he says, having already rejected everyone who questions what he is doing or challenges his opinions. God can no longer do anything with a proud person, or through him. That person has become a fifth columnist, however much he may claim to be fighting evil in the Church and in the world. The true heavenly King, on the other hand, invites his followers to join him in bringing the word of life to everyone. They must know their own need of God, and they are not promised any permanent reward until the battle is over, either in terms of physical or spiritual riches. What the Lord offers now is the invitation to share in the hardships of his own life on earth: poverty, insults and injury to reputation, indignities, misunderstanding and rejection. These are the conditions of a share in his glory. All these things help people to realize their dependence on God for all their daily needs. And God can do anything with people who live in dependence on him because his own power is perfected in weakness.

I related the two progressions that the director had given me with my own experience. He had explained that the enemy tempts people to seek riches, then honour and thence to the pride which cuts people off from God. The true King calls people to poverty, shame, and a real desire for the Christian quality of humility which enables them to hear God's word to them and do it. That helped me see past St Ignatius' picture of medieval knights in armour to the truth of the real warfare I was engaged in. The aim of the day's prayer was to see this so clearly that I could *choose* to be poor in spirit, without wanting any visions or insights in the imagination. Then I would be much less likely to go wrong and think I was superior to everyone else. I could even choose actual physical poverty if it didn't get in the way of what the Lord wanted me to do for him, because actual poverty would keep me aware of my need to trust him for everything. If I could only do that I could rejoice that I was humiliated and put down, because then I should know when I really was following Jesus who had the same treatment from the spiritual and political leaders of his own day.

I was light years away from wanting to be humiliated. I'd begun to see the value of physical poverty in helping people to trust God. The Church in Tanzania was rightly committed to the fight against abject poverty which destroyed people's faith. But I had learned myself that my rich western culture could stop me ever learning what true trust in God was. I could see the value of spiritual poverty too: I didn't usually have the kind of imaginative insight into Christian truth that God was giving me this week, and it would be very easy to credit it to my own spiritual perspicuity and expect it as a matter of course when I got home. That kind of insight was as open to misuse as any other gift of prayer. But was humiliation the answer to that temptation? I'd been humiliated often enough in the past to know that I did not like it at all. But when I thought of the imaginative visions I'd had earlier, of being cut off from Jesus and of the people in their empty circles cut off from God's grace, I realized how close I'd come to being a fatal casualty of pride. I too had rejected people who didn't agree with me, and I too had needed someone else's help to bring me back to God.

102

When I looked at my life in the light of Jesus, I could see how far from Christlike I was. 'I should like to be with Christ in glory,' I thought. 'But I don't like his way of getting there.' That was like the ancient and modern Gnostics, who deny that Christ really suffered physical pain and emotional trauma and conclude that his followers can likewise rise above these things by knowing how to tap into the appropriate currents of spiritual energy. That idea appealed to my imagination much more than taking up the cross to follow Jesus. I wanted to be a spiritual success, not a failure. That was like the ancient and modern Montanists, who couldn't forgive failure. I already knew how hard I found it to forgive failure, in myself or in other people. 'The battle line goes right through the middle of my own life,' I thought. 'I have got to learn how to fight on the right side, under the cross of Christ.'

Knowledge wasn't the same thing as salvation. I might have been given a new insight into the battle going on in the whole Church, but that didn't mean that I was any better than before at fighting on the right side. One of the Scripture readings that the director had given me was the story of Simon the Pharisee who criticized Jesus for accepting the tears and the ointment of a sinful woman (Luke 7. 36-50). My imagination produced a very vivid impression of the story which related it to my own life, but its vividness only served to show how far I was from being able to forgive those who put me down. 'It is the man who has been forgiven little who shows little love,' the Lord had told Simon, and he seemed to be speaking to me as well. He forgives because he is love. If I could not forgive readily, what did that mean? It wasn't only second-century heretics who had problems with forgiveness. A person could be completely orthodox, as Simon was, and fail to forgive because he had never really known his own need of forgiveness.

I went down to the little chapel to pray for help. Community Mass was about to begin and the chapel was full of very elderly men, all wearing black cassocks. It seemed like another world from the past and I felt completely out of place, like a gatecrasher at a party. The Mass was in Latin, mumbled far too fast for either my ears to catch or my limited understanding to translate. The only part of the service I could both hear and understand were two

103

readings in English. The first was a selection from the book of Proverbs:

> The mouth of a wise man is a virtuous fountain, violence lurks in the mouth of the wicked... In the eyes of a fool the way he goes is right, the wise man listens to advice.' (Prov. 10.11; 12.15 JB)

The gospel for the day was the story of the Lord's family coming to see him, an incident which drew forth his words about his true family: 'My mother and my brothers are those who hear the word of God and do it' (Luke 8. 19-21). There are no privileges of status in the Kingdom of God. Even the mother of God was not honoured because she happened to be the one chosen to give him birth, but because she had heard and obeyed.

I had to hear and obey now, I thought. Evangelicals too could see themselves as an élite, just as much as any other group of Christians could, if they thought that they were the only people in the Christian Church to possess the true doctrine of salvation. I had to listen to advice, not think I knew everything already. And yet I did not want to water down the gospel. The English Reformers had insisted that public worship should be carried on in a language everyone understood, because only that way could superstition be avoided. Mumbled Latin was no more intelligible than charismatics all burbling away in tongues. I looked at all the elderly men around me and I thought of what the preachers in my childhood church had said about people who lacked true faith and tried to pull themselves up to God by their own efforts. At the most mumbly part of the Mass, when the celebrant seemed to be talking entirely to himself, my Protestant prejudices finally broke out. 'What *is* all this?' I asked the Lord. His answer came back immediately: 'Do you think that what you say has anything to do with my coming? Any one of these men has more love for me than you do.'

I felt dreadful. I hadn't learned *anything* from all the insights I'd had in my prayer this week. I was still judging other people in the Church as if I were the only Christian to have got everything right. I had seen the causes of what went wrong in the Church today but that didn't turn me into a victorious knight of Christ. I'd been sitting there amusing myself during a liturgy I couldn't understand by comparing the participants to little black-robed gnomes, relics of an ancient mythology from the past. I wouldn't have admitted it, even to myself, but Jesus knew what was in my secret heart. He knew what was in their hearts too. He knew the true value of their dedicated lives and their love for him expressed unobtrusively through years of humble service. They had no great fame or earthly reward: 'jesuitical' was a dictionary adjective for prevarication and intrigue. They had made a lifelong, continuous gift of themselves to the Lord in obedience to his call. And I'd simply written them off.

I too had to hear and obey. It wasn't something I did once for all in a flash of high emotion; it was a daily and hourly commitment to his service for the rest of my life. I could begin now, I thought. I could remember to turn to the Lord in everything, not think I could manage by myself. I could accept not only my circumstances but also my trying moments from his hands, as well as giving thanks for the obviously good things he gave me. I could choose a way of life within my own circumstances of marriage, family and work, that would help me use the gifts that God had given me for his greater glory. I had heard his call to me, to build up and heal and help other people to truth and strength. I had to carry it out. And the Lord's way of carrying it out was the practical way of quiet teaching and humble service, not by making myself out to be a great authority and proclaiming everyone's sins in public and analysing them and making a fuss about what went wrong, as if I never went wrong myself.

'Well,' I thought as I walked back to my room after the service, 'I mustn't get depressed because there isn't any instant sanctity. It would be thoroughly bad for me if I had it. I can only grow in love by being forgiven, and my failures do at least help me recognize my own sin that needs forgiveness. I'm prey to exactly the same temptations as everyone else, and the only reason I haven't fallen flat in public is because the Lord has mercifully denied me the opportunity of standing in the public eye.' I was going to have to become a lot less sensitive to other people's criticism and minor snubs and a lot more sensitive to my own faults, so that I could come to the Lord at once for forgiveness and strength, not wait until I'd got everything so wrong that I needed someone else to sort me out.

Anything can go wrong if Christians judge each other and fail to forgive each other, and perhaps the only way to be able to forgive other people is to recognize what is going on in my own life and the tiny ways I fall daily to the temptations which break other people in publicly visible ways. 'I need to ask the Lord daily for forgiveness,' I thought, turning to him in prayer. 'Forgive me for being angry just now. Forgive me for belittling those people who serve you faithfully. And forgive me for thinking that what I say can help you in any way, when you have died for me.'

Church institutions become oppressive and destructive without the Holy Spirit's fruit of gentleness and love which enables people to forgive. I thought about some of the things I'd seen go wrong. Patterns of discipline and training could put people into strait-jackets and cripple them. 'Spiritual formation' could be a recipe for turning out identical Christian sausages. Worship could become a spectator sport. Preaching turned into entertainment or diatribe. Spiritual direction tore people to shreds and threatened to destroy their faith. Even retreats like this could be used by the enemy to turn people from Jesus if they were not centred on him and carried out in the power of his Spirit, in gentleness, kindness, meekness and humility.

The ancient Gnostics used to give people retreats. They took scriptural passages out of context and presented them for people's imaginative contemplation, and they felt quite free to rewrite Scripture when it suited them. Their aim was to gain insight into their own personalities: who they were, whence they came and whither they were bound. It all sounded quite convicing. But it destroyed people's faith in Jesus because the Gnostics saw no need of forgiveness. Evil was real to them but they saw it as part of the created human condition which spiritual people had to rise above. Evil to them was not a result of human beings deliberately ignoring God's will.

St Irenaeus was a bishop at the time, and he was very concerned about what was happening to his people. He had no earthly power

106

to restrain the Gnostics: the Church itself was seen as an illegal religion by the Roman state. He was learned, and took the trouble to find out what the Gnostics were teaching, but even that was not enough to guard people against them, because the Gnostics came up with new systems of self-analysis quicker than he could warn his flock about the old ones. All he could do was to point out what they were doing and correct it himself. Scripture, he said, was like a mosaic of little glass pieces laid out to make a picture of a glorious king. The Gnostics rearranged the pieces to make a picture of a badly-drawn animal. St Irenaeus described, as well as he could, the true picture of the King to be found in Scripture: the Lord who is true God and true man, who shared our whole human nature, was born into the ordinary conditions of working life and did the will of the Father without wavering. Jesus did God's will completely and perfectly within those conditions until he died a shameful and humiliating death out of love for us all.[2]

That is the true King who calls me to follow him. He is the King at the centre of the *Spiritual Exercises* who called St Ignatius, as he had called St Irenaeus fourteen hundred years before, to make his truth known. That was the King whose portrait in the twentieth century could be altered or obscured. I had been called to the task which his people are engaged in through all ages of history: to make the picture visible again for my own people in my own society. It would take me the rest of my life to do that, in company with all the other members of his body whom he called to do the same.

The day's meditation had, I thought, cured me of wanting to judge by my own standards. I needed God's gift of spiritual discernment and I needed to develop it by constant application to the truth of Scripture. And I was cured of wanting to pass judgement on other people. If there's a war on it is hardly fair to criticize the casualties. Even Gnostics and Montanists, ancient or modern, have their place in God's whole purpose. The Gnostics drew forth St Irenaeus' true picture of Jesus as the centre and head and heart of the whole material and spiritual universe, drawing everything that exists to himself. Then I remembered what Ronald Knox had said in his book *Enthusiasm* about the Montanist movement. It had encouraged the Church to decide at an early stage that human weakness was going to be a perennial problem, and that the commission given by the Lord to his apostles was the commission of the Church: to forgive.

Notes

1. Montanists and Gnostics are described in many books about early Church history, but the accounts I found most helpful were R. Knox, *Enthusiasm* (Oxford 1950), pp. 25-29 on Montanism and R. M. Grant, *Gnosticism and Early Christianity*, New York, Harper Torch Books, 1966. For the modern gnostic movement see T. Roszak, *Where The Wasteland Ends*, Faber 1973; F. Musgrove, *Ecstacy and Holiness*, Methuen 1974.
2. St Irenaeus, *Against The Heresies*, ET F. R. M. Hitchcock, SPCK 1916. The account of the mosaic is in 1.7.5: 'By their perversions and changes, and by making one thing out of another, they deceive many with their specious adaptations of the oracles of the Lord. It is just as if there was a beautiful representation of a king made in a mosaic by a skilled artist, and one altered the arrangement of the pieces of stone into the shape of a dog or fox, and then should assert that this was the original representation of a king. In much the same manner they stitch together old wives' fables, and wresting sayings and parables, however they may, from the context, attempt to fit the oracles of God into their myths.' The answer was to have the rule of truth: the Christian framework of faith, received in the catechetical instruction and sacramental life of the Church (1.9.3).

10 · Means of Grace

The law was given through Moses; grace and truth came through Jesus Christ (JOHN 1.17)

Ignatius saw temptations coming to Christians through the wish for wealth and honour, the temptations of educated society in his day, when even clergy sought high positions of power and good livings. There was also a temptation to reject these obviously 'worldly' temptations and fall for more subtle, spiritual ones: wanting spiritual experience in order to be one of the élite; refusing to admit sin and failure in yourself but blaming everyone else; preferring to concentrate on your own spiritual progress rather than go out in practical humble service to others; failing to relate imagination and rational reflection; failing to see yourself as one part of the whole body. All these things led to pride. Seen like that, insults and rejection began to take on a new value. Being rejected by a society that judged poverty to be a sign of failure wouldn't matter nearly so much, if wanting success in the world's terms was a temptation. And being snubbed by members of a spiritual upper class was a very good thing if it kept your feet on the ground.

But just as attachments to worldly goods can take the negative form of fearing their loss, so attachments to spiritual goods can show up as fear of appearances. That was my own temptation, I thought. I tried every way I could to disguise the fact that I was studying Christian doctrine: I didn't want to look like a 'female intellectual' or a 'female would-be cleric'; it was bad enough being a 'female professional' in some circles. I had often failed to speak out, I realized, because I was simply afraid of what other people would think. But sheltering behind Rob in a phoney 'little woman' mask was no answer at all. If God was calling me, he was calling me as I was and I had to get over this childish desire to please everybody and to be approved of. 'Lord,' I prayed, 'I am not willing to be humiliated. But I am willing to be made willing.' Better

Christians than me had prayed like that before. But I really couldn't pray for any more humiliations: I hadn't got over the last lot yet. Of course I was being oversensitive; I'd told myself so dozens of times. But knowing that didn't make the hurt any better. I hadn't even been able to face thinking about it until another of the biblical passages I'd been given to see how the Lord was rejected had resonated with my own life and brought the painful experience back. Now I knew that it was just sitting there in my inside, like a great whale stranded on the beach. I didn't know what to do about it. Was that really what God wanted? It was quite possible for pride to refuse his assistance in alleviating pain.

I'd had to face this question before, during our first tour in Tanzania, when our office motor cycle was stolen. At that time we lived a long way from the office where we worked and we both felt the strain of walking everywhere in the heat. Carrying the shopping for the family brought on a recurrence of an old trouble I'd had, and I went to see the doctor who asked a few searching questions and prescribed medicine. 'Of course,' she said, 'what you really need is transport.' I'd prayed for the sick for years; I knew that health, along with prosperity and success, is seen in the book of Deuteronomy as God's gift to his people when they turn back to him and re-order their lives according to his will. I knew that Jesus came to bring 'life in abundance'. I was personally involved in a down-to-earth project to help meet people's physical needs. But the link made by the doctor between my own sickness and the practical problem of transport uncovered all sorts of unexpected theological pitfalls. There was no way that we could buy our own car or even a private motor cyle. Cars cost nearly ten times as much in Tanzania as they did in the UK, and we were earning local salaries.

On the way back home from the surgery I met a friend and told her what the doctor had said.

'Well,' she said, 'you'll just have to pray for a car.'

'I can't do that,' I said, horrified. 'If God had wanted us to have a car, he'd have given us one.' She was unconvinced.

'You pray for people when they're ill, don't you?' she argued stoutly. 'You don't say, "If God wanted them to get better they would be." Anyway, even if you won't pray for yourselves, I'm going to pray for a car for you.'

When I got home, I told my husband about this conversation. Could our friend possibly be right? What *was* it that made us feel so strongly that praying for a car was out of the question?

'It's all those American religious paperbacks,' said Rob. 'They pray for a car and get two gold-plated Cadillacs in the next post. It's phoney. "God grants you the American Dream when you pray in faith." I don't want to be a soap-opera Christian.'

'That's not my problem,' I said. 'I don't mind praying for other people, but praying for myself bothers me. Perhaps it's because I know I'm basically selfish, and need to keep battling against wanting everything to go my way. But it can't be that I don't like to admit my needs, because I was quite pleased to be prayed for.'

'It's praying for a *car* that's the trouble,' said Rob. 'Praying for the sick can be quite vague; you can imagine a benign spiritual influence which will help in a general way no matter what the doctors say. But if you pray for a car, you'll either get it or you won't. You can't tell yourself that you've got a "spiritual" car. You have to face the fact that God either has or hasn't answered your prayer.'

'You can leave God right out of "spiritual" prayer,' I confessed. 'I've sometimes caught myself praying as if it was my prayer that was going to help the person, like a kind of telepathic good will. Not God at all.'

'It's much easier on the nerves,' he said. 'The other kind is distinctly uncomfortable. I remember the Vicar who took my confirmation class praying for a road drill to stop because it was disturbing us. I felt awful. If it didn't stop, none of us would ever believe in God again.'

'Did it stop?'

'Yes, it did. The workman must have gone for a break. It started up again just as the class finished.'

'That was lack of faith,' I told him piously. 'The Vicar believed that God would give you the peace and quiet you needed, and you didn't.'

'It was worse than that. I didn't believe that God *could* answer his prayer. I still don't know how he did it.'

'That's our particular way of looking at things, though, isn't it? The "scientific world view". We think we're explaining things when we describe how they work, but it doesn't really explain anything at all.'

'And then we've come from a relatively rich country and been brought up to work for what we need. You'd never dream of praying for a car in England. You'd set about earning enough money to buy one.'

That was my real problem. Why should I pray to God for a car when I ought to be able to stand on my own two feet? When do you give up on human effort and tell God you've had enough? It seemed rather easy to give up too soon; I'd felt very definitely superior to my weaker expatriate brethren who relied on regular air-lifts of imported breakfast cereal and lived in cocooned comfort behind twelve foot high chainlink and barbed wire fencing, patrolled by alsatians to keep their hi-fi equipment intact. I didn't want to give in. I felt that I could identify with the local people on foot. Why couldn't I walk to the market without falling to bits? They had to.

That was the crunch. I simply wasn't as physically fit as I should have liked to be and I had to face the fact that as an expatriate I did not have an extended family to help me. I couldn't even ask the prayers of the Church for my ailment. There was an embarrassing tradition in the English-language Sunday service of giving out detailed prayer requests. I could just imagine the suppressed titters of the congregation if they were told precisely what I was suffering from. There was nothing for it. We should have to pray for a car if I wanted to get better. There was no conceivable means of us buying one. And I did want to get better: the project was at an exciting stage and I was needed in the office.

We prayed for a car. I had met my friend on Friday. It took us until the following Tuesday to overcome our scruples and join our prayers to hers. On Wednesday morning the principal of a professional firm on the coast phoned our office. They were planning to open a branch office in the region: would we do them a favour and look after their Landrover until they moved up? We could of course have the use of it between their visits. On Wednesday afternoon a colleague stopped my husband in the road. He'd been looking everywhere for him; he was going on long leave and his motor cycle had been allocated to us. By Thursday evening the motor cycle and the Landrover were parked outside the house. But we did take the precaution of bringing the motor cycle indoors before we went to bed and immobilizing the Landrover engine. We didn't expect God to do everything for us.

That incident had taught us both to pray definitely for what we needed and to trust God to provide in a concrete way. I wanted to prove to people in Britain that God *did* answer this kind of prayer: but I didn't feel able to pray for better circumstances for myself. Was that the same reluctance that had stopped me praying for a car in Tanzania, or was it a feeling that my real witness was to show by my life that my security didn't rest in material possessions? St Ignatius had said that we should choose what was more to God's glory (*Spiritual Exercises* nos 179 and 185). What was more to his glory in a society that tended to see the acquisition of material goods as the chief end of man: to show that God could provide these things miraculously or to show that he could supply the grace to do without them? I thought I knew the answer, when the question was put like that.

But that didn't answer the question of hurt feelings and humiliations. I had done what I thought God wanted me to do. I'd given practical help where there was an obvious need, I'd served in an official position because I'd been asked to do so, I'd organized some informal worship at home, and I'd helped lead some Bible studies at a small prayer group. That was during our last tour, when I'd also been ill with two consecutive long-running infections and was laid flat with my neck. It had not been an easy tour, but I'd been conscious of the Lord's strength and help in trouble, even when we'd had three burglaries one after the other and lost our camera and various other worldly goods, including most of our warmer clothes. I could have coped with the physical hassle. What had been so difficult to come to terms with was the constant wearing opposition on all fronts to absolutely everything I tried to do. I certainly hadn't set myself up as a leader in the community. I

113

hadn't particularly wanted the glory of doing any of the things I had done. But there were several people who did and they had made life very awkward. Even new arrivals from the UK or elsewhere seemed to have been told about all my shortcomings before they'd even met me. 'Once bitten . . .', I thought. Unless God made it quite clear that this *was* what he wanted, I certainly was not going to ask him for the same kind of opposition again. It was all very well to see humiliations as leading to humility but this was out of all proportion, like using a bulldozer to flatten a sandcastle. I'd been flattened all right but was it all really necessary?

There had indeed been a time when we'd had to swallow our professional pride and learn humility in our working life. Our house help and some other people we knew quite well lived in a roughly built, sprawling village which happened to be right in the middle of an area planned for Government offices. They were all quite naturally concerned about where they would live, and so were all the different departments in our own Government organization. Various schemes for resettling them had been proposed but none of them were quite workable, for various technical reasons: it was a tricky problem which none of us seemed able to solve. But the residents' worry about their future was affecting their lives, and one day we decided to pray about it, although strictly it wasn't our department's concern at all. We might have expected that God would enlighten the minds of those whose proper responsibility it was to deal with the matter, 'those in authority' whom we prayed for on Sundays in the Anglican Church. Instead, when we'd finished praying, Rob and I and the two British volunteers working with us looked at each other. 'I think,' someone ventured, 'that this is something we've got to do something about ourselves.'

We all felt the same, although it didn't make sense. None of us was a qualified planner. Rob and I had done part of a planning course during our architectural training, but neither of us had gone on to the final year, and in any case that was years ago. Not only that, but there was a whole Planning Department at the office and it was *their* job, not ours. 'OK,' I said, 'I don't mind having a go, but I'd rather do it at home out of sight, if you don't mind; it will avoid awkward questions.' But this isn't the way God works. There were people in the Planning Department who were just as concerned as we were and they gave us all the information we needed to make a start. Various specialists arrived seemingly out of the blue to do jobs which were quite unrelated to what we were doing, and one way or another they gave us a great deal of invaluable advice. The head of our own department was also an expatriate at the time and was experienced in cutting through red tape in his own country; he cut through our qualms about official procedures and insisted that once we'd started the job we ought to finish it properly. We finished the plan for a self-build resettlement area the day that questions were asked in the national parliament about the problem. The question reverberated down the chain of command until it reached our department. What were we doing about it? 'Where's that plan?' asked the head of department, bursting into the office. 'The minister's been on the line.'

That plan would have drawn the scorn of any properly qualified planner in this country, because it went right against current planning theory and broke most of the rules. But it was passed because it was appropriate for the particular situation there. Perhaps you have to learn to be 'unskilled' in order to see what the problem really is, I thought. If we hadn't been unskilled, we'd never have taken so much advice from other professionals. There is of course safety in numbers, and there were four of us: but we *had* stuck our necks out and we *had* come in for some criticism. We had weathered it and in the end a large community had been able to build its own housing. It was relatively easy to face opposition in the world. It was much, much harder when it was your fellow Christians who opposed you. I couldn't see any sense in that at all. There had been no achievement at the end of my last tour, because my own illness had stopped me doing practical things and I'd given in over the worship and Bible studies because it didn't seem the sort of thing I should insist on doing if other people in authority didn't want me to. So all the hassle had been for nothing. Rob had been working in the office and finishing off his work with the project, but my last two years had been quite wasted and useless.

All of this came back to mind when the director gave me the subject for the day's prayer: Jesus washing his disciples' feet, and the institution of the Eucharist at the Last Supper. The grace I was to pray for today was compassion: grief with Christ in his suffering. It seemed an odd petition. I found it easier to understand his suggestion that I should link the Last Supper with my own life by thinking in terms of the love that we bring to difficult situations. 'If you don't find love in a situation,' he had told me, 'put love in, so that you may draw love out.' I knew I hadn't done that completely last tour. I'd put love in, but when my love was rejected I'd felt flattened and in the end I'd snarled back at people. There wasn't much point linking *that* with the story of Jesus.

I decided that I would like to go to Mass this morning before I turned again to the Gospel story of the Last Supper. That was real not imaginary. It was participating with other Christians in the Lord's action now, in the present. I'd already asked the director if I could take Communion, and after asking a few questions about my own belief he'd agreed. He would be celebrating mid-morning, he said, and there would be one or two other lay people present. I went down to the chapel early and spent the time before the service praying for the unity of the Church. And during that service, I began to understand what unity really means. It is not a matter of *feeling* united. My devotional euphoria did not outlast the opening sentence.

'This Mass is offered for the soul of . . .' began the celebrant. I took a deep breath. That was what the Reformation had been about. I'd answered all the questions I'd been asked, but the director had never said anything about *that*, and I didn't believe that at all. 'Sacrifices of masses, in the which it was commonly said, that the Priest did offer Christ for the quick and the dead, to have remission of pain and guilt, were blasphemous fables and dangerous deceits.' Article 31 of the Anglican Articles of Religion was quite clear on the subject and it wasn't any use the Anglo-Catholics saying that it referred to medieval aberrations, because all Evangelical Anglicans knew that Cranmer had turned the liturgy inside out to make sure that nobody went away thinking that Christ could be offered. In the Anglican Church it is Christians who offer themselves to God; Jesus offered himself

116

once and for all on the cross, and that can't be repeated. Article 31 was quite clear about that, too.

I'd missed about three pages of the service book. I was reciting the words quite mechanically. But as the service proceeded I was caught up into an overwhelming sense of unity and love with everyone present. It was almost tangible: something given by God and nothing at all to do with me or my own state of mind. The love of Jesus which united us seemed to dissolve my fears that I was betraying the gospel by being here. Jesus is truth. He told his disciples to love one another. All Christians, living and dead, are bound together in the love of Jesus. It was as if I could see the dead person being carried in our love and prayers, as we were all taken up into the greater love of Jesus which cleansed and directed our own human love.

I walked back to my room after the service still surrounded by that sense of unity and love. It was so strong that I followed the others down the wrong stairs and got lost before I found my way back to the right ones. That unity was given by God. It put a whole new complexion on my own understanding of 'sacrifice'. In the service of Holy Communion, Christians affirm that they are the body of Christ: the same body that was broken for us. We offer ourselves to God; but we offer ourselves in union with Jesus because we can't do it on our own. Our offering by itself is not acceptable, because of the sins of the past which continue to shape our lives in the present. But Jesus sets us free and cleanses us from sin. We *are* acceptable when we identify ourselves with his offering of himself for us. But in order to identify ourselves with his offering, it has to be actually present with us now. In the Eucharist, or the Mass, or the Lord's Supper or the Holy Communion, all Christians, living and dead, are united in thanksgiving and intercession with Jesus who has won the victory over sin on our behalf and stands in heaven to intercede for us. And of course we can't offer what he does without offering ourselves at the same time, because in the sacrament he does make us one with himself.

I'm no theologian and I had no idea whether this contradicted the fundamental tenets of Evangelical Anglican belief or not. But it seemed obvious that if we *were* to be united we had to be united in

117

Jesus, and trust him to make us one and set us free from the partial and distorted statements of truth that Christians had made in the past by bringing us into his own truth now. The Hebrews knew more than we do about bringing different insights together in a way that would turn any Greek philosopher's hair white. Logic doesn't have the last word. I'd often wondered why the books of Exodus, Leviticus and Numbers combined to stress the fact that the Israelites' first anniversary of the original Passover deliverance was inextricably bound up with making and setting up the tabernacle, instituting priesthood and sacrifice, and offering the gifts of the people. Now I understood. The glory of God, the writers were saying, has left Mount Sinai and goes with us on our journey, within the institutional life that God has given us for this very purpose.

The writer to the Hebrews translated this vision into New Testament terms (Heb. 12. 18-24). We make our offering not to a remote, terrifying God at the top of a mysterious mountain, but to the living God in the heavenly city of angels and saints past and present. We are cleansed and united in Jesus who has brought a new relationship with God for all mankind. We no longer have to listen for the word of an infinitely distant God, because the Word of God was made flesh and lived among us, and his glory has appeared in visible form, like light shining in darkness, like the fire which led Israel through the night. Perhaps that was the answer to my own experience of darkness, I thought. If I wanted to see the fire of God's love clearly on my journey, I had to accept that there would be darkness behind me as well as ahead. But following the light of love was the only way to the heavenly city where all are made one in Jesus. Could I accept the loss of my past certainties, in order to carry other people with me into that love?

11 · Hope of Glory

For this slight momentary affliction is preparing for us an eternal weight of glory beyond all comparison (2 COR. 4.17)

God's love given to us in Communion is his gift. If I forgot that, I might think that it was *our* human unity and love which enables us to offer the sacrifice of Jesus, not the other way round. Catholics guard against this by the way they word their liturgy and by the rule about confession before Communion. Protestants stress the fact that Christians do not stop being sinners the minute they turn to Christ and it is self-deception to think you no longer have any need of repentance. But I had to admit that the practice of saying that I was a miserable sinner all the time had numbed me to the reality of my sin and the need for practical, definite penitence. Very holy people might be able to cope with a continuous awareness of their sins and respond with unceasing sorrow for them, but I wasn't up to it. Too much liturgical stress on my unworthiness had rather the same effect on me as parental statements of the type: 'Well of course you always *were* noisy/indolent/talkative/untidy.' Most parents do sometimes say this kind of thing to their children; and however hard I try to avoid it I know I often say it myself. It may work as a last resort, and produce the desired result, reducing the noise to a tolerable level, or getting someone to help with the washing-up. But the long-term effect is to discourage people to change for the better.

I needed to change. I had seen that my witty criticisms of other people were symptoms of a deep-seated pride which passed judgement on everybody except me, because it took my own opinions as the standard for everyone else. That pride still stopped me reacting like Jesus when I was under pressure, or when I myself was criticized, or when I was snubbed. That pride had to be attacked at the root. But I didn't know how I could dig it up. It didn't seem like a simple operation of getting to the bottom of a

119

tap-rooted weed and pulling it out in one clean tug. My pride was much more like one of those pernicious weeds like ground-elder which forms a tangled mass of interlocking underground runners, and sprouts immediately from the tiniest bit of root left in the ground. My pride was a matted web that ran through my whole life. I needed a systemic weed-killer in order to begin to deal with it.

'Ask for sorrow, compassion and shame, because the Lord is going to his suffering for my sins.' (*Spiritual Exercises*, no. 193.) The Lord's death for my sins is the only way of dealing with the pride which refuses to acknowledge sin. '*My* sins,' I thought. 'Not "our sins."' It was a lot easier to indulge in vague feelings of guilt about what went wrong in the Church and reproachful regret for the mess mankind had made of the world, than it was to ask for 'sorrow, compassion and shame' for *my* part in the Lord's suffering.

I wanted to make my petition real, not vague, and I decided to reinforce it by climbing the hill where the stations of the cross were carved into the steps. There was a wonderful view from the chapel at the top as I prepared to pray with the gospel story of Jesus washing his disciples' feet. I remembered that sense of love I'd known at Mass this morning: it was like a very much stronger version of the sense of the Lord's compassion that I'd felt as I looked at that same view from the road below the other day. I'd known that love in Tanzania, too, I thought. I'd known it as I prayed and worshipped with other Christians there. I'd betrayed that love by passing judgements on other people: it was rejecting the love of Jesus in them and for them, offending against his body. 'If I'm going to be part of this story,' I thought, 'I ought to be Judas who betrayed the Lord.' Wasn't I still in league with his enemies at heart?

'No,' the Lord said as I thought about it. 'You be Peter who repented of his betrayal. Be Peter and let me wash your feet.'

I was sitting in a canvas garden chair which tilted back as I leaned into it, reminding me of the chair at the dentist where I'd been having dental treatment recently. I didn't want to be reminded about dentists. I hated dental treatment. I'd had too much of it over the years not to feel nervous. I felt nervous now.

'This is going to hurt terribly,' said the Lord, in exactly the same tone of voice as the dentist, only the dentist always says it won't. I knelt down on the floor, and one by one the people I knew came into my mind and I confessed out loud my sins against them as they came to mind: mostly what I'd thought and felt but sometimes what I'd said. It was all dreadfully dreary and boring, and it seemed appropriate to be doing it there on my own in a dark place amidst the bat droppings on the floor. But in the end all the detritus of that painful period had gone, and I knew that I was swept clean inside.

It was a good job that Protestants didn't go in for formal confession, I thought as I walked back to the house. I couldn't imagine anyone having the patience to sit through all that. On the other hand, if I had been more used to making a definite confession of sin in front of someone else as a regular habit, I might not have let it all pile up like that. But at least I now knew that confession could not be superficial. Confession was just like going to the dentist: it could be a protracted and painful ordeal. But it was real, painful confession that had turned my own sorrow from resentment to *true* sorrow for sin. There was still pain and I still couldn't make any sense of it, but the bitterness and the dreadful, demoralizing guilt which had festered like an abscess was no longer there.

Being honest about ordinary human weakness and failure is the bedrock foundation on which the Church is built, because it is the practical proof of faith in Jesus as the Messiah who saves from sin. This is the only way that Jesus saves the world. If I am not willing to let him save me that way, there is no other way that he can save me. God's grace and mercy are given to human beings in the broken body of Christ, making his voluntary weakness and suffering humanity into the food which nourishes believers with the life of God. And *that* is what we are given to share with others. Jesus is the sacrifice for sin who makes us holy: he was, St Paul said, 'made into sin' for us, so that we could become God's goodness (2 Cor. 5.21). 'Once you have recovered,' the Lord told Peter, 'you in your turn must strengthen your brothers' (Luke 22.32 JB). He was to strengthen them not by the example of someone who had never

121

fallen, but by being one who had betrayed his Lord and repented, who had been forgiven and restored. Peter after the resurrection could bear witness to the Lord's mercy because he had known it himself. Paul knew this too; he called himself the 'chief of sinners' because he had once persecuted Christians and sinned against the Lord's body, not knowing what he did. But the Lord had appeared to him, and he had found mercy and broken the confines of his narrow understanding of God's grace to become the apostle to the Gentiles. And he, too, knew that it was the mercy of God that lay at the heart of his message, however great the visions of glory he had been granted. It was his weakness that he boasted about, because the Lord had told him that his grace was enough: 'My power is at its best in weakness' (2 Cor. 12.9 JB).

I still could not see my life in the way that Peter and Paul had seen theirs. I knew that I had to let the power of Jesus' love transform my weakness and failure. But how could I? I wasn't meek in the face of trouble any more than Peter had been at first. My reactions had led to all the sins I'd just spent the afternoon confessing. Unless I could change, my reactions would go on being the same and I should repeat the pattern over and over again, making it even more difficult to keep on loving people when my own love was rejected. My own love simply was not strong enough to cope. The director had said that we could see trouble in a different light by looking at what Jesus did with his suffering. And yet how could I identify with Jesus when he did what nobody else could do and took our sins away by offering himself to the Father in his suffering? The director had said that Christians could bear each other's burdens in this way too. 'Redemptive suffering', he'd called it, and I'd switched off because Protestants don't believe that anyone but Jesus can do that. Was it possible that I'd been wrong?

How could I strengthen the fellow-Christians with whom I disagreed, unless I could understand the conflicts which had hurt me in the light of God's wider purpose for us all? Jesus did not use his power to avoid trouble, much less to destroy his enemies. God's Kingdom does come in power to destroy the chains that cripple people and oppress them and keep them from knowing God's love.

But it comes in stubborn hearts that oppose it by submitting to their rejection, because when God's Kingdom finally does come with power over men's hearts there will be no more time to turn and change and grow. Jesus redeems me and everyone else by making the world's opposition the raw material of his own life-giving sacrifice.

One of the problems that I had about seeing my own troubles like this was that even if they were not the occasion for self-righteous indignation and self-justification, they were still quite trivial compared with what the Lord suffered. And yet, I remembered, the experience I'd had of being rejected and feeling sad as a result had given me a new insight into the Lord's sorrow in the Garden of Gethsemane. My sadness certainly hadn't been as great as his, but it had helped me to understand his love for me better. I'd used my own experience as the basis for a Good Friday meditation on the Lord's sorrow:

> Sorrow is like a sea,
> a midnight tide, rising
> to fill channels first, to join
> over the saltmarsh, slowly to cover
> living creatures breathing below mud,
> whistling grass and stiff sea-lavender,
> rattle and shift of sand and shingle;
> all sounds submerged in silence.
>
> Four fathoms down,
> sorrow has no horizon;
> twenty fathoms down,
> the mind slips sideways, flattens
> edge on to the current, like a flounder;
> a hundred fathoms down,
> light fades to a faint memory of the surface;
> five hundred fathoms down, and further,
> monsters move unseen,
> crusted against destruction.
>
> But, for the unprotected,
> pressure pounds throbbing through every pore,
> hammering skull and skeleton,

squeezing and straining heart's blood,
brain and body battered beyond bearing.

This also you know.

Now, as I remembered that time and how I'd used my relatively shallow experience of suffering in order to enter imaginatively into what was much greater, I wondered whether that was not also the way to look at the Catholic concept of 'redemptive suffering' for each other. Poetry is not prayer, but it can lead in to prayer. Imaginative identification with Jesus is one way in to a deepened prayer which catches up even the trivial hurts of daily life in an offering of love to God. I knew that I was going to have to let Jesus show me my own life in the light not only of his life of ministry, but also of his suffering and death. Could I do *all things* for love of him? The director had reminded me that Jesus redeems us by what he does, not by what he says. 'His redemption is not in his preaching,' he had told me as he outlined the background to the day's prayer. 'It is in his action'. But we didn't call this 'action', I thought. We called it 'the Passion'. Could I let what happened to me be done for love of him too?

Protestants dislike the idea of 'redemptive suffering' because to them it sounds too much like trying to bargain with God. Jesus refused to bargain with his accusers in any way. He kept silence. I didn't want to bargain with my small hurts, either. But more than that, I did not want Jesus to bargain with *me*. It was monstrous to think that I could take on trials voluntarily which nobody had asked me to bear, and try to blackmail God into doing what I wanted on the strength of them. It was no less monstrous to think that Jesus did what he did in order to blackmail me. I thought of the Holman Hunt picture, and my grandmother's expression which had been so like it, and the sermons I'd heard and the hymns I had sung, like the hymn at the end of Stainer's *Crucifixion*, where Jesus seems to be saying, 'I'm doing all this for you; what are you doing for me in return?' And I realized with a shock that I had always thought of salvation in exactly the same terms as I'd thought of tea at Grandma's house when I was a child. I liked being in her house and sitting at her table and eating the food she had prepared for me.

But I was not going to eat the homemade kipper paste, no matter how put out she looked. I never asked her to go to all that trouble. And I never asked Jesus to die for me either. In all these years of wondering what salvation meant, my imagination had never really accepted the salvation that Jesus was offering me.

The Lord must have accepted the fact that I was childish rather than childlike in my understanding of his love for me, because he took me just as I was and showed me the truth at my own elementary level. The scene of his arrest in the garden came to life in my imagination before I had even opened the New Testatment. There was a muddle in the dark, with torches flickering in and out among the trees and people coming and going so that it was impossible to tell who was a disciple and who was making the arrest. Then a disorganized procession formed, with Jesus being hustled along in the centre of a group of officials, and a crowd of ordinary people around them and straggling out behind. I was an onlooker, standing by the roadside, watching. As the procession came up to me, the crowd on my side of the road thinned out, and I could see Jesus quite clearly. He drew level and stopped, turning to face me. He was quite close to me.

'I did this for love of you,' he said. 'What do you do for me?'

Suddenly, all my defences crumpled. It was not a bargain that he was trying to make; it was a simple statement of fact. He did it for me so that I should be set free to respond to his love. And that was all he wanted from me: my love. That was all the response he was asking. He was calling me to grow up and leave behind all my typical childhood fantasies of bargaining or revenge by suffering: 'I'll run away and die in a ditch and *then* you'll be sorry.' He wanted me to follow him in breaking through the barrier of self-justification to see everything that happened as contained within God's purpose and therefore as capable of revealing his love, and he wanted me to accept his love as a gift which would kindle my own.

The procession was about a hundred yards down the road by the time I had gathered my wits. My imagination seemed to be carrying on with the story while my thoughts were otherwise engaged. I found myself back inside the scene, having to run to catch up. By

125

the time I did, Jesus had already been taken inside Annas' palace, and there was a lot of coming and going in the courtyard where the preliminary hearing was taking place. Annas has always stood in my imagination as the typical cynical ecclesiastical politician behind the scenes, manipulating his victims into his hidden networks of power and intrigue like a cunning and ruthless spider. To me, he represented the 'World' within the Church. As I stood there, the crowds parted, and I could see Jesus again, facing me across the open court.

'I do this for love of the World,' he said. Then everyone came outside again, and the crowd straggled across the road, joined by more and more people. The street was full: young and old, rich and poor, honest and shifty, of every racial origin under the sun. Jesus turned to face me again and spoke to me once more.

'I am doing this for love of my children, to draw them to myself.'

I had been thinking of my obedience as something I did for God. I thought of 'Christian service' as something external to myself. But this reversed my view of things. Jesus went through all that indignity of arrest and insults and false accusations and cross-examination for love of me. His love for me was shown then, two thousand years before it ever occurred to me to respond to it. How could I ever again judge anybody else for failing to respond? And how could I think of 'my work' in terms of its visible effects now? I could no longer think of myself or anyone else as 'good' or 'bad', 'worldly' or 'pious', 'spiritual' or 'unspiritual' in the light of Jesus who did what he did for a whole world that killed him. If salvation was a gift I could no longer resent the hostility of those who opposed me or brought my work to nothing through their intrigues. Jesus did what he did for all his children, and I simply do not know how far he has drawn any one particular person to himself. All I can do is allow him to draw *me* to himself, and perhaps use me if he so wills to help the process forward. That would dry up once and for all the root of my judgement on other people, and of wanting to be judged by my own external standards. Jesus has overcome the World by his love. I could trust him to overcome the World in me.

The scene continued to play on in my imagination. I followed the crowd into Pilate's residence, squeezing into the great court with the other bystanders, but I couldn't see Jesus at all. I was wedged behind a wooden crash barrier, with crowds of people in front of me. Once, when the crowd shifted, I caught a glimpse of a figure in a red cloak, a very long way off. I could hear snatches of what was going on, but the people around me were talking, too, and I couldn't catch the drift. People were beginning to call out as the whole crowd gradually edged towards hostility. Then I heard one voice raised clearly over all the rest: ' And who does he think he is, anyway?'

It was the same voice, in the same tone, that I'd heard when I'd walked into a meeting unexpectedly at the end of our last tour, and interrupted someone complaining about me in similar words and in exactly the same voice and tone. 'And who does Anne Netherwood think she is, anyway?' It summed up the failure of that whole period of my life and all my own experience of rejection came flooding back. All the things that people were saying about me during the last two years were what the crowd was saying to Jesus. And I cried and cried: for myself, and for him, and for the waste and futility of it all.

'He bears our griefs and carries our sorrows,' I thought. 'But he doesn't take them away.' I wondered about this, and then the other things started to come back: the crushing sense of failure and worthlessness, and the guilt and the hollow emptiness, and I started to shake with the fear that had possessed me before the director's prayer for me. Then all this suddenly lifted and the Lord was saying, 'Anne, I am taking this away, because that shouldn't be there.' And then I realized that the *other* sorrow was all right. It was the result of trying to do what he had told me to do. And he doesn't take that away, ever, because it is the means by which I could be identified with him in his sorrow for the world. *That* was his gift to me; and I could no longer feel hurt or angry at anyone who had caused it. I could accept that pain as something creative, enabling me to react with his love, not mine, in the world where I was.

The other scenes went on: the procession carrying the cross, the scenes of the crucifixion. But the human reality of pain and suffering got fainter and fainter behind a sort of living wall of love radiating and pulsing out from it all. I couldn't see the crucifixion at all: just the love, like a rippling curtain of golden light, shining with the true light of God's glory from the heart of the cross. The reign of God is fulfilled when the true Servant of the Lord suffers the full injustice and hatred of his fellow-men, accepts it as his because he is part of the human world, and says to the Father, 'Your will, not mine, be done.' That is the ultimate transformation of evil into good. The cross is the final revelation of the love of God, spreading out from that one point in time and space to fill the entire universe with his grace. This is the banner of Christ, under which all his servants enlist, and the work which he calls all his friends to share. The true banner of Christ is the ensign of total, self-giving love, which conquers evil and brings joy, because, as Bernard of Clairvaux knew, 'his fatherly love is greater than any injustice whatsoever.'

12 · The Eighth Day

After the Sabbath, towards the dawn of the first day of the week . . . (MATT. 28.1)

It is five years ago to the day as I write this that I prayed for the grace of the eighth day of retreat for the first time: 'to be glad and rejoice intensely because of the great joy and the glory of Christ our Lord' (*Spiritual Exercises* no. 221). There has been darkness and pain since then, but the joy has not worn off because it is not a surface emotion. The true joy of the resurrection is a deep inner conviction of the truth of the gospel, and that can't possibly wear off because it is eternally true. I was set free during those eight days, five years ago, to follow the Holy Spirit's leading without the fear that had crippled me in the past. I knew I was free when I could see what had happened to me in the light of the Lord's life and death and knew that whatever else he called me to do or to suffer for him must be done in his way. I then had to live in that freedom, allowing the Lord to form me through my daily life as I met him in prayer and in the gospel, recognizing his light in the decisions I had to make, and offering myself to him in the suffering that came my way as a result of putting his calling to me into practice. I have failed many times since then to do this, but I am no less convinced than I was then that this is the only way I can live as a Christian now.

In those five years Ignatian retreats have become very popular with many people outside the Roman Catholic Church or the Anglo-Catholic wing of the Anglican Church. But the effect of a retreat should not be judged by its popularity any more than by the vividness of insight a person gains through it. The only way to measure the effect of any kind of retreat is by the help it gives a person to live the gospel day by day afterwards. My experience as an Evangelical encountering a foreign Christian tradition through making a short retreat was that this tradition supplied an imaginative and doctrinal framework for the Christian truth I already knew from within my own tradition. It gave me the confidence to choose between the different impulses in my mind by comparing the end to which each one led with the Lord I met by praying with the Gospels. It also gave me the confidence to continue to pray without images, in the knowledge that Jesus is the foundation of my whole life: not just his image but his own life which he gave for me and gives to me. And my experience gave me the confidence to follow what I believed to be the Lord's true call to serve him in the Church.

All this brought a great deal of tension and pain which I could have avoided by forgetting about the call of God, as I had done before I made that first retreat. The impulse which led me to pray for reunion between Christians also led me to notice that the Lord's prayer for unity in St John's Gospel is made immediately before his arrest and takes the place of the description of his agony in Gethsemane in the other three Gospels. That knowledge put a new complexion on my own prayer for unity. Real unity is found only through the death of our partial dreams of local messiahship which will give glory to our own particular group. I believe that it is only the knowledge of the joy of resurrection that gives Christians the courage to let go their traditions of the past and the verbal formulae they need to safeguard them, and trust God to raise up again in visible form the body of Christ on earth, now as he has done before. The resurrection of Jesus is the hope of the Church; it is also the hope of the whole world. World and Church are not united until the end of time. Meanwhile the battle goes on as it always did; and the witness that overcomes the world is the same now as it was two thousand years ago.

The joy of the Lord's resurrection helps me live with the tension of knowing that the Holy Spirit leads Christians in different ways and calls them to forms of service which seem from a purely human point of view to be incompatible. The way God was leading me in prayer can be seen as incompatible with a life of witness and service in the world. In his 'Contemplation to achieve love' St Ignatius spoke of the freedom to find God in all things (*Spiritual Exercises* nos 230-237). That freedom entails the tension which comes from having to make real and binding choices about things rather than simply ignoring them. Rob and I did together choose a low-key way of life and we chose not to look for professional status, but that didn't make it any easier to accept the shame of finding oneself a statistic of 'rural poverty' not just because we lived in a substandard house – we took out a mortgage to improve it – but because we were setting up a professional practice from scratch and dependent on Income Support for two years. Having seen the value of actual poverty as a spiritual blessing did make it easier to stick to our course when things were difficult, but it did not lessen the embarrassment of signing the prescription forms at the local chemist or telling the dentist we were officially 'poor'.

I found that making a retreat helped me to follow God's call and live out the gospel in my daily life. Other people manage to do this without going away. I have had to be careful not to extol the advantages of making a retreat in a way that devalues the faithful lifelong habits of Bible reading and devotion to Jesus that have always been at the heart of true Evangelical piety. What that first retreat gave me was a new vision of Jesus not only as central in my own personal life but also as central in the Church of which I am one part. I can no longer see the Evangelicals as the 'true Christians' – if I ever could – because I have seen much more clearly that people follow the Lord's call in many different ways, and there are many more who are genuinely trying to find out what 'follow me' means for them. But I am convinced as never before that prayer and service and witness in the world are not incompatible activities. St Ignatius' 'finding God in all things' helped me to understand better St Paul's 'in everything God works for good with those who love him, who are called according to his purpose' (Romans 8.28). I know that this is true. Whatever the future may hold, a retreat gives me the confidence in God I need now in order to turn and face in the right direction.

Protestants stress God's grace in his choice of them; Catholics stress that God's grace is given to us so that we can work together with him. Both Protestants and Catholics need to see their life with God as dependent on his saving power and directed towards his 'praise, reverence and service'. The Eastern Church links God's grace to his gift of himself in the sacraments of the Church: the penitential tears which are the fruit of baptism; the variegated ministry in love and power which is the fruit of Pentecost; the unity in love which is the life of the Lord within his body, continuing the harvest of his passion of which his resurrection is the first fruit. Perhaps the whole Church needs each part in order to understand God's grace; and perhaps the full extent of that will not be seen until the end of time either. Meanwhile, it seems more appropriate to accept it and co-operate with it than to argue about it. But just because of the arguments, Christians may be tempted to deny their dependence on God's grace and think that they can co-operate in 'work' if not 'worship', because their 'work' can be done in ordinary, secular ways. I am quite convinced that this is not true, and that unless Christians do *all* their work in Christ's way, they have nothing at all to offer the world at large.

'Lord, my heart is not proud,' prayed the psalmist (Ps. 131.1 NEB), and it may have been a prayer to remind kings of their total dependence on God. There is always a tension between realizing the greatness of God's calling and at the same time knowing that it is quite impossible to fulfil it by any human reckoning. Humility is not the same as denying the call of God and burying your one talent in a hole. Humility is living all the time in conscious dependence on God. I'm not humble, but I'm learning; and that retreat did set me on the right road.

Humility is helped greatly by the realization that I am not alone in learning to listen to God. As I was packing up to leave after that first eight days the director came to say goodbye. I thanked him - not adequately - for his help. He asked whether I'd been comfortable in the room I'd been given. 'Oh, yes,' I said, 'I hadn't expected carpets and upholstery and thick blankets; I'd thought it would be a bit more "monastic" than that.'

He chuckled. 'It wasn't like that twenty years ago,' he told me. 'But then, twenty years ago, you wouldn't have been allowed in.'

God had dealt with a few of my prejudices in the eight days. But the community at that retreat house had had to let him deal with theirs for twenty years in order to make it possible. I knew then that the eighth day of retreat isn't the end. There is no final word or perfect vision in this life, but only the way of Jesus which points us all in the right direction.